"Did you know that evergreens were first used to chase away evil spirits? That Santa Claus was probably descended from the norse god Odin?"

—DOROTHY MORRISON

CELEBRATE THE SUN'S REBIRTH

The holidays: some call them Christmas or Hanukkah, others know them as Las Posadas or Ta Chiu. Still others celebrate Winter Solstice or Yule. They are a time for reflection, resolution, and renewal. Whatever our beliefs, the holidays provide us with rituals to celebrate the balance of light and dark, and for welcoming the healing powers of warmth back into our world.

Jam packed with holiday lore, recipes, crafts, rituals, and more, *Yule: A Celebration of Light and Warmth* guides you through the magic of the season. Traveling its realm will bring back the joy you felt as a child—the spirit of warmth and goodwill that lit the long winter nights. Discover the origin of the eight tiny reindeer, brew up some Yuletide coffee, and learn ways to create your own holiday traditions and crafts based on celebrations from a variety of countries and beliefs.

ABOUT THE AUTHOR

Dorothy Morrison is a Wiccan High Priestess of the Georgian Tradition. She founded the Coven of the Crystal Garden in 1986. An avid practitioner of the Ancient Arts for more than twenty years, she teaches the Craft to students throughout the United States and Australia and is a member of the Pagan Poet's Society.

An archer and bow hunter, Dorothy regularly competes in outdoor tournaments and holds titles in several states. Her other interests include Tarot work, magical herbalism, stonework, and computer networking.

TO WRITE TO THE AUTHOR

If you wish to contact the author or would like more information about this book, please write to the author in care of Llewellyn Worldwide and we will forward your request. Both the author and publisher appreciate hearing from you and learning of your enjoyment of this book and how it has helped you. Llewellyn Worldwide cannot guarantee that every letter written to the author can be answered, but all will be forwarded. Please write to:

Dorothy Morrison
℅ Llewellyn Worldwide
P.O. Box 64383, Dept. K496-0
St. Paul, MN 55164-0383, U.S.A.

Please enclose a self-addressed stamped envelope for reply, or $1.00 to cover costs.
If outside U.S.A., enclose international postal reply coupon.

Many of Llewellyn's authors have websites with additional information and resources. For more information, please visit our website at http://www.llewellyn.com

DOROTHY MORRISON

Yule

A Celebration of Light & Warmth

Llewellyn Publications
St. Paul, Minnesota

FIRST EDITION
Fourth Printing, 2004

Book design and editing by Karin Simoneau
Cover design by Anne Marie Garrison
Cover Illustration and Interior Illustrations © 2000 by Kate Thomsson

Library of Congress Cataloging-in-Publication Data
Morrison, Dorothy, 1955–
    Yule: a celebration of light and warmth / by Dorothy Morrison.
        p. cm.
    Includes bibliographical references and index.
    ISBN 1-56718-496-0
    1. Winter solstice. 2. Winter festivals. 3. Christmas. I. Title.

GT4995.W55 M67 2000
394.261—dc21   00-030969

Llewellyn Publications
A Division of Llewellyn Worldwide, Ltd.
P.O. Box 64383, Dept. K496-0
St. Paul, MN 55164-0383, U.S.A.
www.llewellyn.com

Printed in the United States of America

DEDICATION

For my son, Jeremiah; my nieces, Theresa and Beth; their children, Joshua, Justin, Jacob, and Andrew; and for those the world over who dance in step to the tune rendered by the Kings of Holly and Oak.

IN MEMORY OF . . .

Gary Minton—dear friend and charter member of "The Wild Bunch." The warmth of your laughter is sorely missed.

Other Books by Dorothy Morrison

Magical Needlework
Llewellyn Publications, 1998

Everyday Magic
Llewellyn Publications, 1998

In Praise of the Crone: A Celebration of Feminine Maturity
Llewellyn Publications, 1999

The Whimsical Tarot
Deck and book; U.S. Games Systems Inc., 2000

Bud, Blossom & Leaf: A Magical Herb Gardener's Handbook
Llewellyn Publications, 2001

The Craft: A Witch's Book of Shadows
Llewellyn Publications, 2001

The Craft Companion: A Witch's Journal
Llewellyn Publications, 2001

Forthcoming Books

Everyday Tarot Magic
Llewellyn Publications, 2003

CONTENTS

Part II: Preparing for the Yuletide Season

Part III: Gifting, Feasting, and Festing

ACKNOWLEDGMENTS

While the arrival of Yule evokes an exorbitant amount of good will, warmth, and cheer, it also provides us with some other very important opportunities: a time to reflect, a time to count our blessings, and a time to show appreciation for all the wonderful things other people do for us. Such was the case with the writing of this book. Happy holiday memories resurfaced. They brought smiles and caused pause for thought. Blessings flowed freely. I counted each one gratefully. Now, the most joyous opportunity of all—the time to show appreciation—has come. To that end, many heartfelt thank-yous to all of you, but especially to the following folks:

To Pat Monaghan for good advice, for supplying reference materials and information, for allowing me to pick her brain, and for permitting the use of her poem, "Approaching Solstice."

To Donna Sharley for the use of her grandmother's divinity recipe and countless holiday ideas, for being my Monday night coffee buddy, and for always being there to set me back on track no matter how long or shamelessly I whined.

To InaRae Ussack, Trish Telesco, and Sirona Knight for consistently motivating me, and for sharing a wealth of ideas with me for this book.

To Kathy and Florence Pruchnicki, Su Walker, Susan R. Larson, Jacquie Brennan, and Janne Potter (along with the women's Pagan discussion group) for their kind generosity in sharing the Runja, Yule Log, Latke, Dragon's Layer Cake, and Plum Pudding recipes, respectively.

To Wendy Crowe and Jami Shoemaker for generously sharing the living holiday tree tradition and the Purging Ritual, respectively, and for making the world a much nicer place to live.

To Anne Marie Garrison for sharing her family Solstice traditions and for designing the gorgeous cover you see on this book.

To Kitty Laust-Gamarra for sharing her terrific Spanish Turkey Soup Recipe and for her sorcery in handling travel arrangements and cheerfully finding whatever information I need at the drop of a hat—even when the computer's down.

To the Sorceresses Extraordinaire: Karin Simoneau, Kjersti Monson, and Amy Rost-Holz for their fabulous book designs, and for always making me look good in print—no matter how difficult the challenge.

To Nancy Mostad and Ann Kerns for their smiling voices, constant help, and undying patience.

To Carl and Sandra Weschcke for taking a chance on me, believing in me, and consistently treating me like family.

And finally, to Good Ol' St. Nick who, on Christmas day of 1998, managed to deliver Mark—the love of my life—complete with a bottle of wine!

May the Sun always light your way through the darkness, and forever wrap you in the warmth of His gold! The Happiest of Yules to all of you!

PART I

YULE AND ITS PLACE IN OUR HEARTS

APPROACHING SOLSTICE

Yes, friends, the darkness wins, but these
short days so celebrate light:

Today the lemon sunrise lasted a few
hours until sunset, all day the snow

glowed pink and purple in the trees.
This is not a time of black and white,

my friends, outside us. Among us, too,
let's sing what winter forces us to know:

Joy and color bloom despite the night.
We measure warmth by love, not by degrees.

—PATRICIA MONAGHAN

1

THE HISTORY OF YULE: HOW IT ALL BEGAN

AS HUMAN BEINGS, WE ARE a diverse group of people. We come in many sizes, colors, and shapes. We come from different cultures, speak different languages, and practice different religions. Even the food we like to eat varies. Yet, no matter who we are or where we live, one thing remains constant: We all look forward to the winter holidays. By some, they're called Christmas or Hanukkah. By others, Las Posadas or Ta Chiu. Still others call them Winter Solstice, Yule, and lots of other names most of us can't pronounce. Each celebration is a little different, but the main ideas are the same. These holidays provide us with a time for reflection, resolution, and renewal. A time for gift-giving, good will, and kindness. Most important, though, they provide us with rituals to celebrate the balance of light and dark—rituals for welcoming the healing powers of warmth back into our world—and that gives us a common ground that draws us together as a people.

So where did they come from, these holidays that we all celebrate? Contrary to popular belief, they didn't begin with Christmas. Rather, they started over four thousand years ago in ancient Egypt. The occasion? An extravagant party to celebrate the rebirth of Horus—the god who appeared in the sky as a fiery orb each day—the same orb we know today as the Sun. Because the Egyptians honored Horus with a twelve-month calendar, the festival lasted twelve days with each day symbolizing one month.

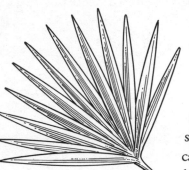

Buildings were decorated with greenery of all sorts to honor the Sun. The most valued decorations, however, were palm branches with twelve fronds. The reason for their value was simple: Because palm branches put out one shoot each month, a twelve-fronded branch formed a type of calendar. This made them a great representation of the entire birth, death, and rebirth cycle of the Sun; using them to honor the Sun was believed to speed His growth and strength, and encourage Him to stay in the sky longer.

The Egyptians flourished, and word of their Sun-welcoming ceremonies quickly swept through Mesopotamia. Believing that the rituals were at the heart of their neighbors' prosperity, the Babylonians took up the cause and got in on the act. However, they called it Zagmuk[1] and incorporated their own Creator/Sun god, Marduk. The Babylonians believed that Marduk had created the world, and made it one of order, beauty, and peace. It hadn't been an easy task, however—first, he'd had to fight a grueling battle and defeat the monsters of chaos.

Each year, everything went along splendidly until the cooler weather brought winter; then the monsters regained their strength and once again challenged Marduk's reign. The battle was on and lasted for twelve days, but Marduk could no longer defeat the monsters by Himself. He needed the help of the people. It was their job to cheer Him on and help Him win the war. Only then could order be restored, and beauty and peace on Earth be renewed.

The Zagmuk festival began five days before Winter Solstice and lasted six days after, with the peak of the festival falling on the Solstice itself. On the seventh day, the Sun stayed in the sky longer—a sure sign that Marduk was well on his way to victory. This resulted in parades on land and river, good tidings, and the occasional exchange of gifts. The world was renewed for another year, and all was right with the Babylonian people.

Not long after, the Persians caught on and began to help Marduk, too. Called *Sacaea*, their festival was a little different and involved a temporary state of chaos. Slaves and masters changed places with each other, a mock king was crowned, and law and order flew right out the window. Grudges and debts were forgotten—if only temporarily. A good time was had by all. And why not? It was the one time of the year that folks could do exactly as they pleased without worry of consequence or retribution. As the Sun's light grew stronger, so did the party. During the last few days, things gradually wound down. By the end of the festival, order was restored to the Greek world.

Eventually, word of these Sun-welcoming festivities spilled into the outside world, and other folks—exchanging Marduk and the monsters for their gods—took up the cause as well. In the Greek version of Sacaea, Zeus defeated Kronos and the Titans, but that wasn't the main reason for their festivities. Apparently, the *Kallikantzaroi*—mischievous imps similar to those defeated by Marduk—roamed the land wreaking havoc during the twelve days of Sacaea. They also had a reputation for stealing the spirits of unsuspecting children, especially those born during that period. Of course, the Greeks did their best to keep them at bay. New babies were wrapped with garlic bundles, and because the monsters supposedly couldn't tolerate fire and smoke, each family kept a large log burning for the duration of the festival. These were fueled with old clothes and shoes, spoiled food, and anything else that might prove offensive to the intruders.

Finally, the ancient Romans—a good many of them practitioners of a Sun-worshipping religion called Mithraism[2]—decided to participate, and that's when the winter festivities really started to take shape. They combined most of the traditions of their predecessors and added a few of their own. First on the agenda was the exchange of god figures—Jupiter for Zeus and Saturn for Kronos. This gave them the opportunity to honor Saturn—one of their most important gods—if only briefly. To that end, the festival was called Saturnalia.

Why all the hubbub about Saturn? Because the god was not only responsible for the pulse of

Nature and its germinating properties, but had gone to great lengths to teach the people about agriculture, fairness, and peaceable living. Commonly known as the Golden Age, His reign allowed fruitful living and the equality of all human beings. With that in mind, it's no wonder that the people jumped at the chance to give Him His due.

The festival began at the Roman temple of Saturn with a ceremony to remove the chains that had bound the god's feet all year long—a sure sign that the Golden Age was alive and well. With that, the whole of Rome was on holiday. Quarrels and arguments were history. Schools were dismissed, and businesses and legal facilities were closed. Because everyone was of equal stature, children ruled families, masters served slaves, and the Lord of Misrule—a mock king—was crowned.

During the week, the Romans decorated their homes and halls with laurel boughs. They lit candles and lamps to chase away evil spirits, and built bonfires on hilltops to encourage the birth of the Sun. The party continued with candlelit processions, singing, masquerade balls, and elaborate feasts. Gift-giving—an occasional practice initiated by the Babylonians—entered the forefront and became a mandatory part of the holiday. The Romans knew how to throw a party, and it was the biggest bash of the year.

As the Sun gained power in the sky, Jupiter once again defeated Saturn. His feet were bound for another year and the order of normal living returned to Rome. But didn't the Romans mind all their fun coming to an end? Not really. After all, Jupiter was the god of success and good health—and one can never have too much of either!

So it went with the popularity of the winter festivals. They spread through Europe, cropping up here and there, taking hold, and gaining power. Eventually, there wasn't a culture, creed, or belief system that couldn't claim their own festival.

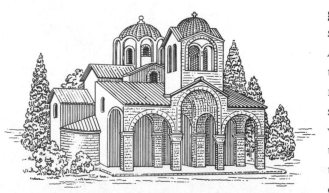

Then Christianity—a new religion—sprang to the forefront and swept through the civilized world. A problem was encountered during the conversion efforts, however. No matter how good the new religion sounded to the Pagan world, they were used to the old ways and their unique lifestyle. Most important, though, they knew how their deities reacted to every situation, and they trusted Them. There was no reason to switch to a form of living they didn't understand, or to a god they didn't know.

Taking that into consideration, the Christians (former Pagans, themselves) devised a plan to make them feel more at ease. First, they built their churches on old Pagan worship sites. Their reasoning was that people had always worshipped on the sites, were comfortable there, and would continue to frequent them, church building or not. They incorporated Pagan symbols within the church decor, and added some revised Pagan customs to their rituals. To help matters further, they changed the names of a few Pagan deities ever so slightly, called them saints, and added them to the Christian pantheon.

It was a great plan, but didn't work as well as originally anticipated. In fact, the Romans didn't take well to it at all. Why? Because they felt that the Christians were making a mockery of their gods. As a result, the Christians were unable to practice safely and went into hiding—for a while—until they could figure out what to do.

Finally, around the fourth century, the Christians had a revelation. Unlike the Pagan religions, theirs was based on the workings of their man-god, Jesus, and his death and resurrection. It had never shown much concern for his birth. Because the birth-death-rebirth cycle had always been a large part of the Pagan belief system, ignoring the birth factor constituted a missing link. Another problem was that the Pagans revered goddesses—mother goddesses in particular. Realizing their errors, the Christians put on their thinking caps and returned to the drawing board.

At last they came up with a series of plans to solve their worship problems. First, they dealt with the goddess issue. Admitting a few goddesses to sainthood wasn't a problem, but they needed something stronger. What they needed was a real Mother Goddess in the midst of their patriarchal world. They finally decided on Mary, the mother of their man-god, Jesus. Previously unimportant to the Christian world, she gained new significance as "the Mother of God." To secure their position, they also played upon her ascension role and billed her as "the Queen of Heaven." This gave Christianity a bit of a safety zone because to the outside world it linked them to Isis, the Egyptian Queen of Heaven.

That didn't solve their problems completely, though. In order to worship safely and gain new members, they needed to meld more evenly with the Pagan practices. Finally, the Christians hit upon a solution: If they couldn't beat the Pagans, they'd simply join them.

Since no one really knew when the Christ-child was born, the Christians set his birthday on December 25.[3] This date fell in the middle of the winter holidays, and because some Pagans held a special celebration on December 25[4] anyway, the new festival would go unnoticed. To ensure smooth sailing, the Christians took an added precaution: They billed the festival as the "Birth of the Son." Because "Son" and "Sun" were pronounced the same, the Pagans would think the new celebration was just an addition to their own festivals. The Pagans were happy, the Christians were comfortable, and Christmas was born unto the world!

NOTES

1. Because historians disagree over the year-end timeline of the Babylonian calendar, some controversy still exists over whether Zagmuk was actually a winter celebration. To that end, I've drawn my conclusions based on substantial material supplied by various sources, including the *New LaRosse Encyclopedia of Mythology* (Middlesex, England: Hamlin Publishers, 1968), *The Golden Bough* (New York: The MacMillan Company, 1951), and the *Encyclopedia Brittanica*.

2. Sir James George Fraser's *The Golden Bough* (New York: The MacMillan Company, 1951).

3. Theologians now agree that Christ could not have been born during the winter. Though viewpoints vary, the most commonly shared has to do with the fact that Bethlehem's winters are brutal—because of this, shepherds only tend flocks at night during the warmer months. During the winter months, they'd have been at home, safely tucked into warm beds.

4. In 273, Roman emperer Aurelianus founded a Sun-worshipping religion called the Cult of Sol Invictus. The birthday of the chief god, Sol Invictus, was celebrated on December 25.

2

Yule Traditions and Symbols

If you're reading this section, you already know that many common Yule symbols and traditions actually originated in Babylon, Persia, Greece, and Rome, but what about the others that we hold near and dear? Things like bells, holly, Christmas trees, candy canes, and Santa Claus? How did they come into being?

Well, even though the Christians managed to convert the masses, a good many Pagans went on with their own festivals; they breathed fresh life into the ancient customs and added new symbols as they went. The Christians devised their own symbologies as well, and pretty soon, all the symbols, customs, and traditions melded together. Figuring out which belonged to whom became a confusing matter, so humankind stepped in and simplified things by making them all a part of the winter celebration. In the final analysis, they reasoned, it didn't really matter which ideas belonged to Paganism or which belonged to Christianity. All that mattered was that they were sacred and belonged to the Yuletide season—a season of diversity and joy—the happiest time of the year.

Be that as it may, it's fun to delve into the origins of things that tell us the holiday season is just around the corner. For example, did you know that evergreens were first used to chase away evil spirits? That Santa Claus was probably descended from the Norse god, Odin? Or that Santa's North Pole dwelling was an American invention? The origins of these and many other common holiday customs follow below.

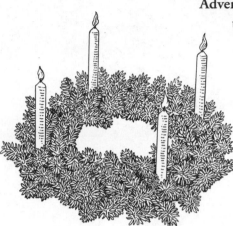

Advent Wreath: Although Advent initially came from the Lutherans, many religious sectors adopted the tradition and adapted its function to suit their own purposes. Traditionally, the wreath is made of evergreens with four candles ensconced within, and its ritual begins four Sundays before Christmas. A candle is lit each Sunday and burns throughout the week to welcome the "light of the world." On the fourth Sunday, all four candles burn together in welcome.

Bells: A throwback to the ancient Pagans, festival participants originally rang bells to drive away the demons that surfaced during the cold, dark time of the year. The Christian bible, however, stated that people should ". . . make a joyful noise to the Lord." Since the tinkle of bells seemed to fit the bill, the tradition of bell-ringing during the holiday season survived and still remains intact today.

Bird's Yule Tree: The bird's tree is a sheaf of wheat, branches of milo maize, ears of corn, or some other sort of grain attached to an outdoor pole or fence post. Traditionally, the tree is set up on Christmas Eve so the birds can enjoy it on Christmas Day. Though this Scandinavian symbol is primarily associated with Christmas and thought to be Christian, its theme is Pagan in nature. The main idea is to share with the animal world and make its members a part of the celebration.

Blowing in the Yule: Although this noisy tradition probably originated as a Pagan means to chase off evil spirits, it's still alive and well today in the Scandinavian and Germanic sections of Europe. In the late hours of Christmas Eve, musicians congregate at the local church and play a carol to each of the four directions. This is orchestrated so they finish at midnight with the ringing of church bells to herald the arrival of Christmas.

Candles: Because fire melted winter's chill and was thought to encourage the Sun to shine, it was always an important part of the ancient winter festivals. Candles, however, are thought to have originated with the ancient Romans who gave them to each other as Saturnalia gifts. Their brightness was thought to chase away dark winter demons and urge the Sun back into the sky. In later years, the Christians embraced them as symbols of Christ, the Light of the World; hence they became a large part of the Christmas celebrations we know today.

Candy Cane: Peppermint leaf and peppermint tea has long been a part of Yule celebrations for Pagans with its coolness symbolizing winter and its heat symbolizing the Sun. The candy cane, however, was invented by an American confectioner who based its form and appearance on Christian roots. He formed it of white candy to signify the virgin birth, then shaped it in a "J" to represent Jesus. The never-ending red stripe was to have symbolized the blood shed on the cross. In spite of the inventor's painstaking creativity and religious devotion, though, the cane somehow wound up as a common holiday symbol and treat—devoid of all Christian testimony and witness.

Carols: These holiday songs are said to have originated from the Catholic Church during the fourth century. The religious repertoire continued to grow through the Middle Ages up until the Renaissance period. The nature of these songs continued to be religious until sometime in the nineteenth century, when European composers began to incorporate other holiday symbols and customs into their music.

Chimney: Santa's descent down the chimney first originated in England. The reason? Santa had to come and go in secret, otherwise no gifts would be left. This tradition was brought to America by the Pilgrims, and still thrives today. (Apparently, German and Scandinavian Santa Clauses don't have to be sooty to leave gifts; it's okay for them to come in and out of the front door!)

Christmas Cards: This tradition was initiated in England in 1843 by a man named Sir Henry Cole. That year, artist J. C. Horsely designed one card and printed a thousand copies. In 1875, the tradition arose in America when Louis Prang printed some cards in Roxbury, Massachusetts. Wanting to make them more popular, Prang then held card design contests. The winners walked away with cash, and the tradition of American Christmas card mailings was born.

Elves: There are several reasons why elves may have come to be associated with the winter holidays. For one thing, the land of elves (Alfaheimr) was inhabited by the spirits who created the Sun, and including these beings in the festival would certainly encourage them to rejuvenate the Sun and make it shine again. A more Yulish theory, though, has to do with Odin the Elf King, whose magical capabilities were incorporated into the Santa Claus we know today. More than likely, the elves were thrown in for good measure to complete Santa's persona. After all, what's an elf king without elves?

Evergreens: Decorating with evergreens dates back to the earliest winter festivals. Because the green never faded from their branches and leaves, evergreens were thought to have power over death and destruction—enough power to defeat whatever winter demons roamed the Earth, and enough tenacity to urge the coming of the Sun.

Gift Exchange: Thought to have originated in Babylonia with Zagmuk, the tradition of gift exchange gained great popularity during the Roman Saturnalia festivals. In later years, the Christians took up this custom as well, but attributed it to the Magi and their bringing of gifts to the Christ-child.

Gingerbread: The Crusaders were originally responsible for this holiday treat, for they introduced ginger to eleventh century Europe on their return from the Middle East. The cookie-like substance didn't become popular during the winter, though, until French and German bakers united and formed gingerbread guilds during the fifteenth century. In those days there were strict laws regarding specialty breads, and since gingerbread was categorized as such, its production was only allowed during Easter and Christmas. Because bakers always had stalls in the European Christmas markets—and no Easter marketplace existed—its spicy flavor and heavenly scent soon became associated with the winter holidays.

Holly: Since holly sports vibrant green leaves and bright red berries during winter's deathly chill, it provides an excellent symbol of rebirth. The prickly shrub was a favorite amulet among early Europeans, and they often placed it in their homes to rid themselves of negative entities and nasty weather. The British have their own holiday tradition concerning the plant, though; since the thorny-leaved plants are considered male and the smooth are known as female, the variety first brought into the house during the holidays determines which gender shall head the household during the next year.

Lights: For centuries, homes and holiday trees were decorated with candles to frighten negative entities and urge the Sun to shine. Although the candles were beautiful, the practice was dangerous; it meant that people had to keep a constant watch to make sure nothing caught on fire. In 1895, an American named Ralph E. Morris finally came up with a solution; he hung some strings of switchboard lights on his tree, and electric holiday lighting was born.

Mistletoe: Although attributed to the Celts—the Druids, more specifically—historians agree that mistletoe was probably first used in the Greek winter ceremonies. When the holidays spread throughout Europe, though, the Druids gave the parasitic plant sacredness and new meaning. For them, the berried plant symbolized the semen of the god, and was used to bring about great fertility and abundance. Hung over the doorway, it also protected from thunder, lightning, and malicious evil. How did we come to kiss under the mistletoe? Norse legend has it that Frigg (the mother of Balder) loved Her son so much that She couldn't bear the thought of something happening to Him. She made a pact with the four Elements that nothing in Their realms would do Him harm. Loki (the God of Mayhem) was up to His regular mischief, however. He fashioned an arrow from mistletoe and gave it to Balder's blind brother. At Loki's instruction, the arrow was shot and Balder fell dead. The wash of Frigg's tears restored Her son to life, and She was so happy that She declared the mistletoe a plant of luck, love, and promise. Since ancient times, people have been kissing under the mistletoe—some of them unwittingly—to receive Frigg's blessings.

North Pole: Aside from the fact that Santa has to live somewhere—and that he appears publicly only in the wintertime—his icy, native home is said to be an American inclusion of no particular significance. After pondering the matter, though, the death-rebirth symbolism becomes apparent in Santa's affiliation with the North Pole. For one thing, the land he lives in is dark and cold; so cold, in fact, that nothing could ever survive its bitterness. Yet, the kindest, jolliest man in the world not only lives there happily, but brings warmth and joy to the hearts of everyone else on the planet. Looking at it from this angle, it becomes apparent that the Sun (Santa Claus) is born each winter and thrives against its chill (the North Pole)—one of the ideas upon which the Winter Solstice celebration is based.

Ornaments: The Germanic peoples originally decorated their trees with fruit, candy, cookies, and flowers. These ornaments symbolized the abundance to come when the Sun shed His warmth. While a lovely custom, the decorations  were heavy and difficult to keep on the tree. After a few years, the area glassblowers put their heads together and came up with a solution: They could decorate trees with the lightweight glass orbs they produced. The use of the orbs made tree decorating an easy process. Even better, the round, three-dimensional shape of the ornaments replicated the shape of the Sun; this provided Pagans with a simple way to honor it—even in the Christian world.

Plum Pudding: Plum pudding is an odd name for this dish, considering that it isn't a pudding, contains no plums at all, and is prepared more for fortunetelling than for eating. A stew, the mixture contains raisins and meat and is laced with spiced brandy and rum. In seventeenth century England, preparing the dish was a family affair; each household member stirred the pot and made a wish. At one point in the preparations, several items—a ring, a coin, a button, and a thimble—were added to the pot. What did they represent? The ring stood for marriage, the coin for wealth, and the button and the thimble were symbols of the eternal bachelor and spinster, respectively. What if one of the items wound up in your serving? Why, it foretold your personal status for the coming year!

Poinsettia: Known for centuries as the Flower of the Holy Night, the poinsettia is the product of an old Mexican myth. Apparently, a young boy wanted very much to give the Christ-child a birthday gift. He was very poor, though, and couldn't afford to buy Him anything. His intentions were so sincere that the Divine intervened and—voilà!—the flower sprang up at his feet. During the nineteenth century, Dr. Joel R. Poinsett—America's Mexican ambassador and an amateur botanist—became so interested in the flowers that he brought some back to the United States with him. Eventually, the plants were renamed after him, and the poinsettia was born.

Reindeer: Although commonly associated with Santa Claus, many people believe that reindeer represent the stags that drew the chariot of the Norse gift-giving goddess, Freya. Another notion is that they symbolize the abundance of the Celtic horned god, Cernunnos. No matter how you slice it, though, the presence of the horned, hooved beasts during the holidays definitely has Pagan origins.

Santa Claus: Although often associated with the Norse Sun-god, Kris Kringle, the initial origins of Santa's capabilities probably had much to do with the myths surrounding the Aryan god, Odin, Lord of the Winds. Legend contends that He was a nocturnal god capable of flying through the stormiest clouds on His gray eight-legged horse, materializing and vanishing at will, and that he held the whole of magic—even its forbidden secrets—in the palm of his hand. Such origin explains why Santa flies through the sky, is never seen, knows who's been naughty and nice, and has a bag of toys that never runs dry.

Sleigh: Santa's sleigh is more than likely a holdover from the Norse myth of Freya. Legend has it that every year She spent the twelve days immediately following the Solstice giving gifts to the nice and doling out misery to the naughty. Her mode of transportation? Why, a chariot drawn by stags, of course!

Snowflake: Because winter brings snow in many areas, it only stands to reason that the snowflake would become a common holiday symbol, right? Well, maybe. There's more to it than that: according to legend, the snowflake was formed from the tears that Demeter cried after Persephone's descent into the Underworld. The microscopic flakes have six sides, and since six is the numerological digit associated with affection, the snowflake was used by Pagans as a winter symbol of love.

Stockings: Although we often think of stockings as a normal part of the winter holiday decorations, they didn't start out that way. Legend has it that three young ladies of meager means were terribly distraught over the probability of their impending spinsterhoods. The problem? They had no dowries and in those days, no dowry meant no marriage. Somehow, word of their angst reached St. Nick. For two nights, he tossed bags of gold through their window. On the third night, however, all the windows and doors were locked. Not to be deterred, he climbed down the chimney and filled the stockings they'd left by the hearth to dry. This legend seems to be the first account of St. Nick being the Santa-like figure we know him as today.

Tinsel and Icicles: The tradition of placing tinsel and foil icicles on holiday trees came from a seasonal story of unknown origins. The gist of it was that spiders weren't allowed anywhere near the tree—not even close enough to take a peek. Upset at this discriminatory practice, they whined to the Christ-child. Once the baby allowed their admittance, they climbed into the tree and covered it with webs. He was so delighted with their creativity that he turned the webs into strands of silver.

Tree: Even though the use of evergreens dates back to the Greeks and Romans, the use of the holiday tree is said to have originated in eighth century Germany. Legend has it that the Christian St. Boniface was trying to convert a group of Druids. Try as he might, though, he couldn't convince them that the oak tree was neither sacred nor invincible. In desperation, he finally cut one down. When the tree fell, it crushed everything in its path but a single evergreen sapling. Boniface declared it a miracle, then proclaimed that the fir tree belonged to the Christ-child. After that, trees were brought into homes as holiday decorations. It wasn't until the sixteenth century, however, that the Germans thought to decorate the branches. Some historians say that the first ornaments— fruit, nuts, and cookies—were used as offerings to thank the spirit of the tree.

Twelve Days of Christmas: The custom of holding a twelve-day winter festival probably began with the ancient Egyptian Sun celebration, and then continued with the Babylonian Zagmuk. (Modern-day historians also allude to the fact that the twelve-day celebration may have originally been designed to honor the zodiacal wheel.) Be that as it may, the church reinvented the twelve-day custom when the holiday was Christianized. Instead of revolving around the twelve days of Solstice, their festival commenced on December 25 (the Christ-child's new birthday) and continued through Epiphany, or January 6, which was the day the gift-laden Magi supposedly arrived in Bethlehem. During the Middle Ages, gift-giving on each of the festival days became tradition. This custom was the basis for the popular carol, "The Twelve Days of Christmas."

Wassail: The original name of an apple orchard fertility ritual, the term "wassail" came to us from the Anglo-Saxons and means to hail or salute. The actual ritual was a matter of saluting the trees and sprinkling them with a mixture of eggs and apples to which wine, ale, or cider was added. This consecration was believed to increase the apple yield for the coming year.

Wreath: Long before Christianity, the circle shape was the primary Pagan symbol of life everlasting—the never-ending cycle of birth, death, and rebirth. It was often used to represent the Sun as well. It's little wonder then, that the Greeks utilized this shape, covered it with greenery, and incorporated it in the decor for the Sacaea fesitival. When the Romans first formed the Saturnalia celebration, they took up the custom, too, but also gave wreaths as gifts to symbolize the infinity of goodwill, friendship, and joyfulness.

Yule Log: Although normally attributed to the Scandinavian peoples, it might be said that the Yule log actually originated with the ancient Greeks, who burned whole trees in an effort to hold off the mischievous Kallikantzaroi. However, the Celts reinvented the custom, and gave it a whole new meaning. The log (a symbol of their Oak King) adorned with traditional evergreens (a representation of the the Holly King) signifies the death of darkness and the warmth of the Sun during the newly born solar year. According to tradition, the log should burn continuously for twelve days, and a bit of the wood should be saved to start the next year's fire. The first day of the Yule fire varies depending upon religious belief. Pagans usually light the Yule fire on the Winter Solstice, while Christians wait until Christmas day.

3

FESTIVALS OF LIGHT
AROUND THE WORLD

MUCH HAS CHANGED SINCE THE first Winter Solstice celebration that was held four thousand years ago. It's evolved, been reinvented, and renamed. We've modernized it, personalized it, added new traditions, and spread it throughout the world. Yet one thing remains constant: No matter how you look at it, the winter holidays still revolve around the balance between light and dark. Each one of them is still, in its own special way, a festival that bids adieu to darkness and welcomes the light—the light that warms our spirits, rejuvenates our bodies, and shows us the way on our personal paths.

CHRISTMAS

(December 25)

Originally intended as a religious holiday to blend in with the Pagan Sun-welcoming rituals and commemorate the birth of the Christ-child, this festival was purposely placed within the Winter Solstice celebration time frame. Aside from the incorporation of Christendom's Holy Family, most of this festival still retains its original Pagan roots. Traditions vary from country to country, but nearly all cultures incorporate trees, decorations, feasting, gift-giving, goodwill, a Santa figure and, of course, lights of some sort.

HANUKKAH

This Jewish celebration meaning "festival of lights" is held in December (dates vary), lasts for eight days, and commemorates the defeat of the Syrians who refused to allow proper Judaic worship. Hence, Hanukkah is a celebration of religious freedom.

What does that have to do with lights? Well, it seems that after the Syrians had destroyed the Holy Temple, a group of religious freedom fighters known as the Maccabees decided they'd had enough. They took on the Syrians, overthrew them, then entered the temple ruins to rededicate it. There was only a smidgen of oil left to light the menorah (the Rabbi's lamp). However, the lamp managed to burn brightly for eight days—the time it took for another oil supply to arrive.

Today's Hanukkah festival still centers around a candelabra with eight candles, called a menorah, with one candle being lit each evening at sunset. The participants play games, sing songs, exchange gifts, and feast on traditional Jewish foods like latkes (potato pancakes) and sufganiyot (donuts). Due to the holiday connection with oil, though, nearly all fried foods are popular treats during this festival.

KWANZAA

Founded in 1966 and celebrated on varying dates in December, this Afro-American festival of lights is fairly new to the winter holiday season. Kwanzaa is celebrated for eight days, with each of the first seven days taking the tone of a different principle to promote positive living. The principles are as follows: unity, self-determination, collective work and responsibility, cooperative economics, purpose, creativity, and faith.

Kwanzaa involves the use of a kinara (a candelabra that holds eight candles); the kinara symbolizes the matrix from which all Africans spring. One candle is lit each day to represent that day's principle. On the eighth day, a great feast is held, all the candles burn brightly, and the tone of the celebration turns to ancestor remembrance.

YULE
(WINTER SOLSTICE)

Yule—a variation of the Scandinavian word *Jul,* meaning wheel—is observed on the first day of winter, the shortest day of the year. One of the common themes during this celebration comes from the Celts. It's the battle between the aging Holly King (representing the darkness of the old year) and the young Oak King (symbolizing the light of the new year). Sometimes the battle is reenacted during ritual. More often than not, though, the tale is simply told while lighting the Yule log in an effort to welcome the Sun, to encourage its easy birth, and to persuade it to cast its warming, healing rays upon our bodies, hearts, and spirits. Although Solstice traditions vary around the world, all of them include light and fire. In Iran, for example, a Solstice celebration called Yalda or Sada involves keeping vigils through the night as seaside fires burn to encourage the Sun to defeat its alter ego, Darkness. Some Germanic peoples still light a fire on this night to honor Bertha—sometimes called "Hertha"—a Sun goddess who tends to home and hearth. (For other Winter Solstice traditions, see the Winter Holiday Customs Around the World section.)

4

Holiday Customs Around the World

Nearly every country has a unique way of celebrating Yule. Customs, rituals, and traditions differ greatly the world over, which makes this winter holiday all the more fascinating. Let's explore how some countries observe the occasion.

Argentina

Santa doesn't visit children in Argentina. Instead, Father Christmas takes over the gift-giving duties, but it's said that he only visits families who go to a little trouble to prepare for his coming. The well-prepared festoon their homes with garlands of red and white and grace their doorsteps with pairs of oversized boots—boots large enough to fit Father Christmas—and make him feel at home. Those who really want to win his favors go one step further, though—they use his image as the top for their holiday tree. After all, what holiday gift-giver could resist that?

Australia

Since the continent of Australia rests deep in the southern hemisphere, its winter holidays aren't filled with the joys of snow and ice and sleigh rides. It's summer there, so Australians check in their coats and scarves for something more in keeping with the weather: shorts, tank tops, and swimsuits. Even Santa follows suit with the summer theme, frequently arriving by way of surfboard or dingy!

Although picnics replace the formal Christmas dinner and beach outings are the norm instead of cold weather activities, the presence of the holiday is still strong and felt by all. Trees are decorated, homes are adorned with a flowering plant called Christmas Bush, and gifts are exchanged. Every year on Christmas Eve, a program called "Carols by Candlelight" is held in Melbourne. At dusk, literally thousands of people gather to light their candles and lift their voices in unison to the world.

China

Since China is predominantly Pagan, only a small part of the population actually celebrates Christmas. Paper makes up the bulk of their decorations, so their homes and Christmas trees (called "Trees of Light") are adorned with paper lanterns, chains, and flowers. Muslin stockings are hung by children in hopes that Dun Che Lao Ren (Christmas Old Man) will visit and fill them with gifts and goodies.

Be that as it may, the main winter celebration comes toward the end of January in the form of Chinese New Year. This festival is held to honor the ancestors, and most of the customs we associate with the winter holidays—gift-giving, lavish meals, lights, and fireworks—are observed then.

Czechoslovakia

According to my Czechoslovakian grandmother, animals always grabbed the Christmas Eve limelight in her childhood home. This practice stemmed from an ancient belief that the manger animals were the most giving of the creatures involved in the Christ-child's birth; so much so, in fact, that they were blessed with magical powers that reveal themselves each Christmas Eve. Still a custom in Czechoslovakia, animals are fed exceptionally well and given an extra dose of tender loving care on that night. Sometimes, even barnyard animals are allowed to stay in the house.

Denmark

In Denmark, the main holiday dinner is held at midnight on Christmas Eve and everyone looks forward to dessert. Why? Because rice pudding graced with a single almond is served, and whoever gets the almond is said to have exceptionally good fortune for the next year. Children leave rice pudding or milk out for Julemanden (Santa) and the Juul Nisse (elves who dwell in the attics of their homes). After all, Julemanden and the Juul Nisse are busy this time of year, and good children ensure that they are given proper nourishment so they can keep up with those hectic holiday schedules!

Greece

Many ancient winter customs are still observed in Greece, particularly when it comes to protecting against the Killantzaroi; for example, the hearth fires still burn continuously for a number of days. The only difference is that the time period now ranges from Christmas Day to January 6. Another protective measure involves fresh basil attached to a wooden cross. The device is kept in a bowl of water and used to asperge the home on a daily basis.

Gifts are exchanged when St. Nicholas—the patron saint of sailors—makes his appearance on Christmas Day, but the big gift exchange comes on January 1. Why? It's St. Basil's Day—a time of renewal, when all the water containers are emptied and refilled in his honor. Gift-giving on this day represents the renewal of friendship, honor, and good will among the people.

India

The Moslems and Hindus of India celebrate the return of the light by placing oil lamps on their rooftops. To encourage the Sun to shine, homes are decorated with plant materials such as banana and mango leaves and flowers of the season. These remind the Sun that He is a valuable part of existence and without His help, all of Nature would cease to flourish. Gift exchange during this time is customary, as well as a practice called "baksheesh," which is a charitable contribution to the country's poor.

Iraq

On Christmas Eve, a bonfire of thorn bush is lit outdoors. Everyone sings to encourage the fire to burn. Why? Because the fire that burns to ashes denotes good luck in the coming year. When the fire goes out, each person takes a turn making a wish and then jumps over the ashes three times.

Ireland

On Christmas Eve, the Irish always put a candle in the window to help light the way of Mary and Joseph, and any other travellers who might happen by. They also place bread and milk on the table and leave their doors unlocked to accommodate those in time of need.

Most of the Irish fun is had on St. Stephen's Day (December 26) when children mimic the ancient custom of hunting the wren. They go door to door with a toy wren on a stick, sing an appropriate song, and ask for treats.

Italy

Most Italian winter festivities fall on January 6 when children await the arrival of La Befana (the Russians call her Babouschka), the kind, old, lantern-holding witch. According to Italian legend, the Magi stopped at her home to beg food and shelter. She refused them and shut the door. By the time she decided she'd been rude and changed her mind, the Magi were nowhere to be found. It's said that she journeys the Earth looking for the Christ-child, and that the never-ending bag of gifts she carries—and shares with Italian children—is His birthday present.

Mexico

Las Posadas brings a flurry of excitement to cities in this country. Market stalls are set up and decorated nearly a month before the big day, and merchants come from miles around just to sell their wares. Then on December 16, townsfolk divide into two groups—the pilgrims and the innkeepers—to play a game that lasts until Christmas Day. The pilgrims form daily processions through town reenacting the journey of the holy family into Bethlehem. They knock on every door asking for shelter. Of course, the innkeepers refuse. One undisclosed home, however, holds a nativity scene and altar. When the pilgrims reach that home, they gain entrance and all join to say a prayer. Afterward, there is a huge party with dancing and feasting, and—as is the case with most Mexican celebrations—piñatas for the children.

Netherlands

Sinterklaas—the Dutch equivalent of Santa Claus—doesn't fly through the air in a reindeer-drawn sleigh on Christmas Eve. Instead, he and his servant, Black Peter, arrive in Amsterdam on the last Saturday in November. Even better, they take a steamboat! They parade through town, then set up their headquarters in a local hotel. All children—royal and common, naughty and nice—must account to Sinterklaas for their behavior during the past year. Gifts are then exchanged on December 5, St. Nicholas Day Eve.

Norway

In Norway on Christmas Eve, businesses close promptly at 4:00 P.M. This gives the townsfolk time to clean up and don new clothes before the coming of sunset heralds the holiday season. Traditional rice pudding with a single almond (a symbol of good luck) is served, but the first bowl is taken to the barn. Why? Because it ensures that the barn elf will continue his watch over the animals in his care. After the meal, the Yule Log is lit to encourage the coming of Julesvenn, who not only brings gifts, but hides barley sheaves throughout the house for good luck. December 26 is the day that children really have fun, though. They put on costumes and play a game called Julebukk that involves going door to door and asking for treats.

Pakistan

For the people of Pakistan, Winter Solstice is celebrated under the name of Chaomos. It's a time of purification, when a messenger of the supreme deity, Dezao, comes to collect prayers from the people. Everyone is symbolically cleansed by a ritual bath for the coming of the light, then all boys and men gather to be sprinkled with goat's blood (another form of purification). Afterward, a huge bonfire is lit to encourage the messenger's departure and the quick blessing of Dezao on His people.

Romania

An interesting winter fertility ritual in Romania involves a sweet, kneaded pastry called "turta." In the middle of kneading the dough, the lady of the house stops and follows her husband outside to the orchard. Since the trees are dormant, he threatens to cut them down. She begs they be spared by saying something like: "Oh no! I'm sure these trees will be as laden with fruit in the spring as my hands are with dough this day!" The trees live, the turta is baked, and pastries are doled out to each family member to eat in honor of the trees and the coming light that will make them grow.

Scotland

Except for the traditional hearth fire on Christmas Eve—lit so the elves can't come down the chimney and cause mischief—most of the winter holiday revelry is reserved for Hogmanay, or January 1. This is the day for "first-footing." Apparently, Scots believe that the first person to set foot in a home in the New Year greatly affects their future luck, and that a stranger brings the best fortune of all. For this reason, most Scots hire a stranger to walk through their house on Hogmanay. There is feasting, singing, dancing, and game-playing after the ceremony.

Sweden

No one really knows why, but sometime around the tenth century, a Swedish king proclaimed that the winter holidays would begin on December 13 (the feast of St. Lucia) and last until January 13. This holiday is called Luciadagen. Beginning on St. Lucia Day, the oldest daughter in each family dons a white dress with a red sash, and places a wreath of candles on her head to signifying the growing light. She takes a breakfast tray of hot saffroned yeast rolls and coffee to her parents' room while her brothers and sisters follow in candlelit procession.

Syria

While most kids look forward to a visit from Santa or one of his kinfolk at this time of the year, Syrian children would much rather see a camel. Why? Because it delivers the bulk of their holiday gifts. This tradition was born of an ancient legend involving the journey of the Magi to Bethlehem. Evidently, there was one small camel in the pack that accompanied them. He wasn't as strong as the others, and had difficulty keeping up. He grew tired, weak, and sick, but wanted to see the Christ-child so badly that he kept pushing forward. By the time he reached Bethlehem, he was nearly dead. The story goes that his determination so delighted the baby that he gave the camel the gift of immortality. Now he returns each year laden with gifts for good Syrian girls and boys.

Venezuela

It's customary in Venezuela to attend daybreak church services each morning from December 16 through December 24. This custom has a twist, however. The traditional mode of holiday travel isn't a car, a truck, or even a pair of walking shoes. It's roller skates! A game is played that is guaranteed to shake things up a bit: At bedtime, children tie a long string to their big toe and hang the loose end out the window. The next morning, skaters are given free rein to tug on any strings still hanging as they make their way to church.

5

OMENS, SUPERSTITIONS, AND OTHER MAGICAL GOODIES

JUST AS WITH ANY OTHER important event, superstition, omen, and augury cling to the winter holidays just like steel to a magnet. A few of my favorites are listed below. If you're interested in finding others, the Internet and your local library are excellent sources.

ANIMALS

- Legend has it that animals can speak on Christmas Eve. Don't listen for them, though—the same legend says it's unlucky to hear them!

- Some cattle ranchers believe that if the first person to cross the threshold on Christmas Eve is female, only heifers will be born on the ranch during the next year. However, if the "first-footer" is a man, many male calves will be born.

• Feeding a sprig of mistletoe to the first cow to bear a calf in the New Year ensures future fertility for both the cow and calf.

• In some parts of Britain, it's believed that if ivy leaves are fed to each cow after milking but before noon on Christmas morning, the devil is forced to stay away from the herd and its keepers for the next twelve months.

• If the stars shine brightly on Christmas Eve, hens will lay well during the coming year.

MONSTERS, TROLLS, IMPS, AND UGLIES

• In Greece, it's customary to burn all old shoes; this will supposedly ward off misfortune in the new year. The shoe-burning custom is most likely a throwback to the ancient Greek family bonfires used to frighten the Kallikantzaroi away.

• In Sweden, it's believed that trolls travel freely through the countryside from dusk on Christmas Eve until dawn on Christmas morning. For this reason, it is common practice in Sweden to stay indoors during those hours.

• In Greece and Poland, it's considered unlucky to be born on Christmas Eve or Christmas Day. Why? Because the roaming monsters—Kallikantzaroi (Greece) and werewolves (Poland)—can easily capture the newborn's spirit and use it to their own devices.

• Ghosts refuse to come out of hiding on Christmas Day. Because of this, it's said that babies born on this day are forever free of ghostly troubles.

Food and Consumables

- If you refuse to eat mincemeat pie on Christmas, you will have bad luck in the coming year.

- If your friends are important to you, you must eat plum pudding during the holiday season; otherwise, you will lose a friend before the next Christmas.

- To ensure your good health, eat an apple at midnight on Christmas Eve.

- After eating supper on Christmas Eve, leave a loaf of bread on the table. This guarantees plenty of bread in the household for the coming year.

- To ensure good fortune in the coming year, Christmas cakes must remain uncut until December 24; even then, one piece must remain uneaten until after Christmas Day.

- In Germany, it's customary to eat lots of greasy pancakes on Winter Solstice, then leave a few on the table to feed the Winter Hag. What if you forget to leave them? Legend has it that the oversight insults the Hag and makes Her very angry—so angry, in fact, that She'll hunt you down, slice open your belly, and take the cakes right out. Why all the grease? There's a reason for that, too. Apparently, it makes the belly so slick that the Hag's knife slides right off—and no matter how hard She tries, She can't harm you or take your pancakes away!

Gift-giving

- If you're planning to give clothing as a holiday gift, take care not to wash and iron it first. Doing so washes away good luck and presses in bad.

HEARTH AND HOME

- To be free of evil spirits, make sure all the fires in your home continue to burn throughout the Yuletide season.

- To bring harmony to the home, some Scandinavian families place all their shoes together side by side on Christmas Eve.

- If you have holes in your stockings, hang them on the hearth before going to bed on Christmas Eve. It's said that St. Nick will repair them once he puts the gifts in place.

- To determine the kind of luck you'll have in the coming year, place a cherry tree branch in water two weeks before Christmas. Good luck is yours if the branch blossoms by Christmas Day.

- If there's a hole in your roof, wait until after January 1 to fix it. It's said that the hole will reappear if you so much as try to repair it between Christmas and New Year's Day.

- It's bad luck to bring holly into the home before Christmas Eve. Bad luck triples if you remove it from the home before January 6.

- Once mistletoe is hung in the home, it must stay in place for one year to ensure good luck. When replaced, the initial piece should be burned.

- Never throw away decorations made of evergreens; they must be burned to ensure good luck (with the exception of holly).

- An ancient German custom dictates that nothing with wheels—especially spinning wheels—may be used from the five days before the Solstice until the sixth day after. Why? Apparently, such action insults the Sun who, at that time of the year, appears to be motionless in the sky. If one insists on spinning during that time, it's said that the Sun becomes so furious that He causes all fleece and fiber to tangle beyond repair.

Marriage Omens

- In Germany, girls play a popular holiday game in which they form a circle around a blindfolded goose. Supposedly, the first girl to be touched by the goose will marry before the rest of the game participants.

- On Christmas Eve in England, it's common practice for unmarried girls to knock on the hen house door. She'll be married within the next twelve months if a rooster answers her by crowing.

- In Poland, it's believed that unmarried women can ensure a quick marriage if they grind poppy seed on Christmas Eve.

- Want to see your future lover? Just toss twelve sage leaves on Christmas Eve winds to make the image materialize.

- In Northern Europe, some unmarried girls arrange three buckets of water in their bedrooms, then pin three sprigs of holly to their nightgowns before retiring. Supposedly, they're awakened by three loud shouts and three boisterous chuckles, followed by the apparition of their future husbands. If the buckets are rearranged, there will be a marriage proposal with no ensuing problems; if not, the future husband may not be a willing partner.

Weather

- Summer harvest will be abundant if the night sky on Christmas Eve is clear and starry.

- The weather on each of the twelve days of Christmas foretells the weather for each calendar month of the coming year. For example, if the first day of Christmas is bitterly cold, the month of January will be bitterly cold.

- If snow doesn't fall on Christmas, the following Easter will be cold.

- A breezy Christmas day brings good luck throughout the coming year.

6

YULETIDE TRIVIA AND FUN FACTS

SO YOU THINK YOU KNOW all there is to know about Yule? The history and origins and how certain traditions and delights came to be? Test your knowledge by reading some of the fun facts below—you may be surprised!

- Modern-day astronomers say that the famous Star of Bethlehem wasn't a star at all. More than likely, it was either a comet or an astronomical phenomenon caused by the conjunction of several planets at once.

- According to historical records, the first American Christmas festivities took place in Jamestown in 1607. The celebration was a device to cheer up the forty settlers who had survived living in the New World. (The original number was one hundred.)

- Because the British Parliament felt Christmas was a heathen holiday, they officially abolished all related festivities in 1643.

• The historical records of 1836 show Alabama as the first state in the Union to give Christmas the status of legal holiday. Oklahoma was the last state to conform; they didn't declare it a legal holiday until 1907.

• The first commemorative Christmas stamp was issued in Austria in 1937.

• Donder (not Donner), which means thunder, was the original name of the reindeer who helped pull Santa's sleigh on Christmas Eve. He was paired with Blitzen, whose name means lightning.

• The story of Rudolph the Red-Nosed Reindeer was written specifically as a sales gimmick for the Montgomery Ward Company in 1939 by one of their employees, Robert L. May. The little book was given freely to every customer who shopped there during the holiday season.

• The candy cane first gained popularity in churches, where it was given as a treat to children who behaved themselves during services.

• Eggnog wasn't always the creamy, rich drink we know today. It's a derivative of a seventeenth century ale called "nog." The Irish celebrated each Christmas Eve by drinking a pint or so, for in their country all pubs were closed on Christmas Day.

• Gingerbread houses became popular holiday gifts during the nineteenth century after The Brothers Grimm released the story of Hansel and Gretel.

• St. Francis of Assisi introduced the singing of carols to holiday church services.

• The first American carol—a song entitled "Jesus is Born"—was written by Reverend John de Brebeur in 1649.

• At midnight on the Christmas Eve of 1914, German gunfire suddenly halted and was replaced by the singing of carols. At daybreak, the German soldiers began to call out "Merry Christmas" to their foes. Before long, both sides declared a truce, shook hands with each other, and exchanged gifts of food, cigarettes, and liquor. The merriment and goodwill lasted for three days.

• Irving Berlin wrote the popular carol "I'm Dreaming of a White Christmas" in 1942 specifically for the movie *Holiday Inn,* in which Bing Crosby starred.

- Two years after World War II ended, the people of Oslo, Norway sent a holiday tree to the city of Westminster in appreciation of British support. This tradition continues today.

- Along the shores of the Mississippi River—especially along the Louisiana coastline—bonfires are lit on Christmas Eve. Their purpose is to guide the way for Father Christmas.

- The image of Santa as we know it today was popularized by none other than the Coca-Cola Company.

- The custom of Santa eating cookies on Christmas Eve originated in Germany where trees were decorated with fruit, flowers, and sweet confections. After leaving gifts for good children, he'd simply help himself to the goodies on the tree!

- Santa's fur-trimmed suit, his cap, and his cloak were fashioned after the clothing of the Dutch saint, Nicholas, who wore a bishop's mitre and vestments.

- St. Nick doesn't get a vacation after the winter holidays. Since he's also the patron saint responsible for Greece, Russia, sailors, merchants, pawnbrokers, bakers, prisoners, children, and wolves, he's a very busy spirit year 'round.

PART II

PREPARING FOR THE YULETIDE SEASON

YULE FIRE

Kindle the Christmas Brand and then
Till Sunneset let it burne;
When quencht then lay it up agen,
Till Christmas next returne.
Part must be kept where with to tend
The Christmas log next yeare;
And weher 'tis safely kept the Fiend,
Can do no mischiefe there.

—UNKNOWN

7

MAKING ROOM FOR YULE

WHEN MOST FOLKS THINK ABOUT down-and-dirty cleaning jobs—the kind that would benefit from a host of white tornadoes—spring usually comes to mind. That's because the season stirs feelings of personal growth and evokes the need for all-around freshness. I'm a little different, though. I like to clean my home thoroughly just before Yule. Why? Because nothing—not even getting the almond in the pudding—guarantees success in the New Year like getting rid of the old year's dirt, dust, and negative energy. Besides, to be successful you must think that way; how can you think success if you've got yesterday's trash clouding your brain?

Granted, it's usually much too cold at Yule to open the windows and air the house, but nothing says you can't handle everything else. I usually turn my success cleaning into a small, informal ritual. It reminds me that the scrubbing at hand is more than simple dirt removal; I'm making room for the wealth of good fortune and other great stuff just waiting to enter my life.

Cleaning Ritual

There's no need to call the Quarters or cast a Circle for this ritual. There's no need for special incenses or candles. In fact, my ritual is so informal that it has no real structure. For that reason, I've provided a marginal out-line below. Use it as a guideline and don't hesitate to add your personal preferences and style. Once you gather your cleaning supplies and get into the business of grime-busting, your personal ritual will fall into place; so will your success in the coming year.

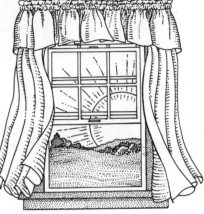

- Start by going through your belongings. If you can't wear it, eat it, or use it, get rid of it. As you sort, visualize any worn-out thought patterns, perceptions, or notions that block your success being tossed into the discard pile.

- Place all your house clutter into a basket or box before you start cleaning. Put everything back in place after the scrubbing is done.

- Grab the broom and use it to free ceilings and walls of dirt and cobwebs. As you sweep, sing the following chant to the tune of "Mary Had a Little Lamb."

> *As I sweep and sing this song*
> *Useless stuff be now gone*
> *Clear out now—you cannot stay*
> *Make room for brighter days*

Continue sweeping and singing until baseboards, windowsills, and floors are dust-free, too.

- Pull down the curtains (unless they are marked "dry clean only") and toss them in the washer. Tie a tablespoon of thyme in an old sock and add it to the rinse cycle. As the curtains rinse, chant something like:

Rinse away the blocks in life
Rinse away all stress and strife
Replace the void with happiness
And prepare the way for new success

- Toss dry-cleanables into the dryer for a few minutes with a "thyme" sock and a damp towel. This will remove all dust. Say the chant above and substitute the word "blow" for "rinse."

- Use an old fabric gardening glove to clean blinds. Just slip it on, dip your fingers in the cleaner described below, and wipe the slats.

- Make an infusion of lemon balm or lemon verbena. (The juice and rind of a whole lemon may be substituted for the herbs if necessary.) Just add one cup of herb to three cups of boiling water, steep for ten minutes, and strain. As the mixture steeps, chant something like:

Lemon herb fresh and lemon herb tart
Dissolve negative energy—make it part
From all that comes within your reach
Clear out old energy, I beseech

Add one cup of the solution to an oil-based soap, then use it to strip grime from baseboards, doors, windowsills, and woodwork. Add a second cup to mop water. Pour the rest into a spray bottle of multi-purpose cleaner and use it to clean walls, surface areas, toilets, bath tubs, and sinks.

- Clean the mirrors in your home. Don't bother with glass cleaner, though; instead, grab the rubbing alcohol. It strips away dirt and nicotine much better than ammonia, and nothing else comes close when clearing negative energy. As you apply the alcohol, say something like:

Alcohol, cut through life's mess
Reflect instead newfound success

Wipe dry with old newspapers.

- Rugs and carpets are favorite hiding places for negative energy. For that reason, sprinkle them thoroughly with baking soda before vacuuming. As you vacuum, chant something like:

> *Negative energy, you cannot hide*
> *I suck you up from deep inside*
> *The places where you grow and breed*
> *Be gone from here—my words now heed*

- Sometimes negative entities take up residence in the home. Getting rid of them isn't as difficult as you may think; all you need is the proper bait. Just place onion slices in small, uncovered containers filled with cider vinegar, then place one dish in each room. As you put them in place, chant something like:

> *I call on your proclivity*
> *To suck up negativity*
> *And grab whatever blocks the way*
> *Of my success in every day*

When the onion turns brown, it's a sure sign that the entity is caught—hook, line, and sinker. Flush the contents down the toilet. (If the slices are too large to flush, simply release them into a body of water.)

- To seal home portals (drains and toilets), squeeze the juice of half a lemon into each one. As you squeeze, say something like:

> *I seal this portal good and tight*
> *Against negative energy's nasty blight*
> *It can't seep through here anymore*
> *With this juice, I seal the door*

Toss the rinds down the garbage disposal or throw them in the compost pile.

- Prevent further negativity intrusion by smudging the home with a mixture of sage and pine. Don't worry if you can't find smudge sticks in that combination; just burn some sage (the kind you have in your kitchen cabinet is fine) and pine needles on a charcoal block, and let the smoke fill each room of the house. As you enter each room to smudge it, chant something like:

Pine and sage, my helpful friends
Protect me and mine from negative ends
Block all but positive energy
As I will, so mote it be

- To keep the house smelling fresh and clean, boil one-half cup of pine or spruce needles in three cups of water for five minutes. Strain out needles and add the solution to a gallon of cold water. Pour into a spray bottle and mist every room in your house.

GENERAL SUCCESS CHARM

Once everything is fresh and clean, it's a good idea to make a general good fortune charm. This keeps the success magic going all year long, and seems to work especially well when hung inside the house over the front door.

UCCESS CHARM

6 inches square yellow fabric
1 teaspoon dried chamomile
1 penny
1 teaspoon dried lavender
1 teaspoon dried basil
1 sprig mistletoe
  A bit of hair or fingernail clipping from
    each person who lives in your home
12 inches yellow ribbon
  White candle
  Frankincense incense

Place the fabric square on the altar, then light the incense and candle. Lay the penny in the center of the square and place the mistletoe on top; say something like:

A penny for luck so money can grow
With good fortune and power from this mistletoe

Add the hair or fingernail clippings. Visualize each person in your home as you add their offering. See them becoming successful in reaching their goals and dreams. As you add each offering, say something like:

> I add (person's name) to this charm to ensure his/her success
> In dreams and endeavors and true happiness

Then sprinkle the dried herbs on top while chanting:

> Oh, herbs now protect and invoke what we need
> Fertilize our success—let it blossom and seed

Gather the corners of the fabric together to make a pouch and secure it with the ribbon. Watch the candle flame for a few moments while you visualize the rays of the Sun pouring down everyone in your household. Then ask the Sun to bless your home and all who live there by saying something like:

> Fire of Sun with light so warm
> With good fortune, our lives now charm
> Open possibilities
> And windows of opportunity
> Fill our environment with new success
> And with positive energy, this home please bless

Let the candle burn all the way down, then hang the charm over the front door. Replace it the following year and toss the old charm in the Yule fire.

Alleviating Success Blockers During the Year

Now that you've created an environment conducive to personal success, you're all set, right? Well, not exactly. No matter how much you clean or how powerful your success charm is, minor negativity can still creep in and obstruct good fortune. There's no need to worry, though. The preventative measures below will help you to stay on top of things and ensure the even flow of the success you deserve.

• If you open a cabinet door or drawer, remember to close it promptly. This keeps people from gossiping about you and causing personal aggravation.

- Know where your broom is. If a guest in your home makes you uncomfortable, excuse yourself and stand the broom bristles up. They will leave promptly and take their negative energy with them.

- Make sure all toilet seats are in the down position when not in use. This keeps both personal and household cash from slipping away.

- Open drapes and curtains during daylight hours. Negative energy hates sunshine and won't live where it's likely to filter in.

- Keep a bayberry candle burning. It not only keeps negative energy at bay, but draws money into the household.

8

DECKING THE HALLS

THERE'S NOTHING QUITE LIKE DECORATING for the winter holidays. Not only is it fun, it also signals the psyche that magic is afoot and gives us a great opportunity to weave that magic through our homes, our lives, and our spirits. Best of all, the world doesn't know that our decorating frenzy is different from anyone else's—and that carries a magic all its own.

THE YULE LOG

When it comes to decorating, one of the first things I like to do is to work on the Yule log. (This is an oak log I chose on the last Winter Solstice and left by the fireplace to dry for this year's celebration.) No need to despair if you didn't think ahead; you can still choose a log and have it ready for Yule. Don't worry if you don't have a place to burn it.

There are two ways to celebrate with the Yule log, and instructions for both are listed below.

Making the traditional Yule log is easy. All you need is a large piece of oak, small pine cones, some evergreens (holly, fir, pine, or spruce snippets work nicely), a hot glue gun, and a length of red ribbon. Starting from the log center, work with the greenery and cones until you have an arrangement that suits you. When you like the placement, attach it to the log with hot glue. Then tie the ribbon around the log to form a bow in the center. If you like, write personal wishes for the new year on little slips of paper, and insert them sporadically under the foliage. Put the log aside until Yule.

When the time comes to burn the log, light it while chanting something to Honor both the Oak and Holly Kings. (If you're at a loss, try the chant suggested in the Personal Traditions section.) For extra luck in the coming year, make sure to keep the Yule fire going for twelve days. After the twelfth day, place some of the ash in a jar with a tight lid. These ashes are very magical, and can be used to boost spellwork in the coming year. Save the rest to sprinkle in your garden or flower beds—the ashes make terrific fertilizer.

If burning wood isn't feasible where you live, a symbolic Yule log is in order. Find a small oak log and carve out or drill twelve holes in the top surface to represent the months of the year. The holes should be large enough and deep enough to support candle tapers. Place the tapers in the holes. (To ensure the candles stand straight and don't topple, I like to use sticky wax candle fittings. They're readily available at any arts and crafts store.) Decorate it as you would for the traditional log, but omit the wish slips.

When Winter Solstice comes 'round, begin by using the chant suggested in the Personal Traditions section. Then light the first taper and say something like:

We give you life, O flame so bright
Return to us your joyful light

Have every family member write a wish and light it from the candle while chanting something like:

Wish flame and flicker, burn and glow
Fly straight into the cosmos so
That you are granted now to me
As I will, so mote it be

Place the paper in a fireproof dish to burn out. Let the candle burn down as far as possible without catching the log on fire. Continue the process each day for the next eleven days, but on the last day, make only personal wishes for the Earth, Her good, and Her environment.

Quick and Easy Yule Decorations

Once the Yule log is ready, turn your home into a magical wonderland. Get into the holiday spirit by decorating mantles, shelves, walls, and corners. Afraid it will be too expensive? Think again! The magical ideas below make great decorations without making short work of your pocketbook.

Evergreen Wreath

Metal ring (the desired size of the wreath)
Sprigs of pine, spruce, fir, cedar, or holly
Pine cones, berries, and assorted nuts (optional)
Thin floral wire
Ribbon
Hot glue gun
Wire cutters

Separate the evergreen snippets into tiny bunches of three or four sprigs. Then wrap the bottom of each bunch with a 6- to 8-inch piece of floral wire. (Wrap from the center of the wire so the ends are left loose.)

Place one bunch on the ring, and secure it by wrapping the wire ends tightly around the ring. Place the head of the next bunch over the bottom of the first and wind its wire around the ring. Continue in this fashion until the entire ring is covered. While you work, chant something like:

Pictured clockwise from top: Evergreen Garlands, Evergreen Wreath, Ina Rae's Yule Centerpiece, Quick Yule Stockings, Placemats, Holiday Harmony Tree, Mistletoe Ball.

Leaves of everlasting life
Leaves that know no stress and strife
Protect us with your perfect ring
Until the Sun this season brings

Arrange pine cones and nuts in bunches around the wreath and hot glue them in place. Cut another 8-inch length of wire for a hanger, fold it in half, and twist the ends around the top of the wreath. Cover the wire with the ribbon and tie the ends to form a bow. Hang it on the front door or in a prominent spot in your home.

 EVERGREEN GARLANDS

Sprigs of evergreens
Thin floral wire
Ribbon (optional)
Pruning shears

Separate the sprigs into bunches and secure with wire as suggested for the Evergreen Wreath. Place one bunch over another so it covers the wire on the bottom bunch. Twist the wire tails of the first bunch around the second to secure it. Add another bunch and wrap the tails of the previous bunch around it. Continue to add bunches in this manner until the garland reaches the desired length. As you work, chant something like:

Long lasting chain of evergreen
Protect from things seen and unseen
Positive energy, please secure
So love and happiness may endure

When the garland is finished, tie lengths of ribbon into bows and attach them with wire at the planned scallop points.

Mistletoe Ball

1 foam ball 4 inches in diameter (florist's foam works best,
     but styrofoam will do)
    Mistletoe sprigs (fresh or dried)
    Holly sprigs (fresh or dried)
½ yard ⅝-inch red ribbon
1 yard ¼-inch red ribbon
    Straight pins

Wind the ⅝-inch ribbon around the ornament vertically, pin in place, and cut. Start from the bottom of the band and wind the ribbon around the ornament horizontally to divide the ball in half again. Pin in place and cut. The ball should now be divided into four equal vertical sections.

Fill in the sections by pressing sprig stems into the foam. Continue until each section is completely covered. As you work, chant something like:

Mistletoe! Holly! Magical Ones!
Bring us joy—add to our fun
May those who kiss beneath this ball
Be lucky through Winter, Spring, Summer, and Fall

Cut an 8-inch length from the 1/4-inch ribbon and form a loop to hang the ball. Secure it to the top of the ball with pins. Then cut the remaining 1/4-inch ribbon in half. Use it to make two multi-looped bows. Pin one bow to the ball top and the other to the bottom.

Ana Rae's Yule Centerpiece

2 identical clear wine glasses or champagne flutes
    Small dried or silk flowers and greenery
    Yule symbols (tiny bells, runes, Sun symbols)
    Small red candle
    Floral clay
    Clear quick-dry glue
    Red ribbon
    Fancy braid (optional)

Place a small amount of floral clay in the bottom of one glass. Push the candle in its center, then arrange the flowers, greenery, and symbols around it. When the arrangement suits you, dot the top of the glass rim with glue. Position the rim of the other glass on top, and hold it in place for a few seconds—just long enough for the glue to set.

Tie the ribbon around the base and fashion it into a fancy bow. Glue the braid around the joining point if desired. Enchant the centerpiece by saying something like:

Symbols of Yule, of long life, and Sun
I bless you with joy and laughter and fun
I bless you with wisdom, good fortune, and cheer
Impart these new gifts to all who sit near

Holiday Harmony Tree

1–2 small thick magazines (Reader's Digest works well for this)
    Gold spray paint (optional)
    Glitter (optional)
    Star, sun, and moon sequin shapes (optional)
    White glue
    1½-inch round ornament

Hold the upper righthand corner of each individual page and bring it down to the center spine of the magazine. Press the fold flat with your fingers. Repeat until each page is folded; include the front and back covers. As you work, chant something like:

Pages of paper, you once were wood
And proudly in the forest stood
I give you back the form of tree
I thank you, paper—blessed be

Glue the covers together. (For a fuller tree, use two magazines and glue the front and back covers together.) Spray with paint and sprinkle with glitter. Add a few sequins if you like. Apply some glue to the center of the tree top, then insert the stem of the ornament. Enchant the centerpiece by saying something like:

Tree that glitters—tree of light
Tree that glistens in the night
Tree that changes constantly
Protect our family harmony

PLACEMATS

Red or green fabric
Old holiday cards and momentos
Clear contact paper
Pinking shears
Scissors

Decide on the size of the placemat, then using the scissors, cut the fabric to the appropriate dimensions. Using the fabric pieces as patterns, cut two sheets of contact paper for each placemat. Cut out pictures from old greeting cards and arrange them on the fabric pieces. Add mementos from previous holidays if you like. When you like the arrangement, carefully peel the backing from one sheet of contact paper and lay it over the arrangement; be careful to work out all creases and air bubbles. Add a sheet of contact paper to the other side as well. Repeat the process for each placemat, then trim the edges with pinking shears. Enchant the placemats by saying something like:

Bits of happiness and cheer
Bring old joys back to us here
Help make new memories as we share
Our dinner table and its fare

QUICK YULE STOCKINGS

Purchased stockings
Felt in assorted colors
Lettering stencils
Fusible webbing
Pen
Iron
Scissors

Stencil the letters of a name on the felt—I like to use a different color for each letter—and cut them out. Using the package directions, iron the letters onto fusible webbing and cut them out. Remove the webbing backing and iron them onto the stocking. If you like, you can also draw Yule symbols, runes, or other designs on the felt and fuse them to the stockings in the same manner. Dedicate the stocking to the Yule King by saying something like:

> *Yuletide King, I welcome You*
> *And Your light, so fresh and new*
> *Bless (stocking owner's name) now with Your love*
> *And guide his/her path from up above*

If you still have some bare spots in your home once the decorating's done, try some of the ideas below for quick yet attractive fillers.

- Turn a picture window into a holiday calendar with a can or two of artificial snow. Use a yardstick to divide the window into columns and rows, then stencil in numbers for dates. Stencil in holiday shapes and figures, too, if you like. Finish the window with a border of lights.

- Hang bundles of foil icicles over door knobs, then secure with a twist tie. Tie a ribbon bow over the twist tie to cover.

- To adorn a bare end table, mantle, or kitchen island, make an arrangement of glass or satin ornaments and ribbon bows in a clear footed bowl.

- To decorate a small alcove, string small glass and satin ornaments on lengths of ribbon or monofilament and hang from ceiling hooks. These look great when suspended from hanging lamps and chandeliers, too.

- Spruce up mirrors, windows, and doorways with strands of colored mini-lights; the lights that have strands that hang freely from a base strand are especially pretty.

- Festoon bedposts, headboards, and footboards with evergreen garlands and bows.

- Secure evergreen garlands over doorways, then add a few candy canes or cookie cutter ornaments (see directions in the Tree Ornament section).

- Arrange some greenery—holly, evergreen snippets, or mistletoe—around the bases of large pillar candles, and set them in various groupings about the house.

- Apples make great candle holders, too. Just remove the core, hollow out, and insert votive candles or small pillars.

YULETIDE CRAFTS FOR CHILDREN

So you've worked yourself into a decorating frenzy. Things look good, but you've run out of ideas and still don't have enough material to finish decorating your home. What now? If you have children, ask them to put on their thinking caps and help you resolve the problem. (If they draw a blank, have them check out the Yuletide Crafts for Children section.) This serves several purposes. For one thing, it gives them an opportunity to exercise their imaginations—a source that is as creatively fresh as it is vast. For another, it allows you—the tired and busy parent—to tap into and make use of their unbridled energy. Most important—at least from this parent's point of view—it keeps kids entertained while giving them a purpose. And we all know that busy children are happy children!

Pictured clockwise from top: Christmas Card Holder, Flower Pot Bells, Stocking Identifiers, Window Snowflakes, Easy-to-Make Sun-Catcher, Hand Print Wreath, Santa Claus Candle Holder.

Easy-to-Make Sun-Catcher

    Wax crayons
2 sheets waxed paper
2 sheets black construction paper
    Large paper bag
    Saucer
    Compass, pencil, pencil sharpener, hole punch, and scissors
    Glue or paste
    Ribbon
    Iron

Place the saucer on a sheet of construction paper. Trace around it with a pencil and cut it out. Repeat with the second sheet and with the waxed paper. (You'll have two construction paper circles and two waxed paper circles.) Place the compass point in the center of each construction paper shape and draw a circle about ½ inch smaller than its measurement. Cut out the centers.

Place one waxed paper circle on top of the paper bag. Insert different color crayons into the pencil sharpener and twist, allowing the shavings to fall onto the circles. Arrange the colors so there are small mounds of each with a bit of space between. When you're satisfied with the color combinations, place the second waxed paper circle on top.

Plug in the iron and set the temperature to medium. Slide the iron over the waxed paper circles until the crayons melt between the two. Allow to cool for a minute or two, then glue a construction paper border to the front and back. Punch a hole in the top, thread the ribbon through, and tie it in a bow. Hang in a sunny window.

Christmas Card Holder

1 evergreen or tinsel garland the desired
    length of the holder
  Wooden clothespins (one for each card
    you want to display)
  Green construction paper
  White glue
  Red glitter

Begin by cutting out two holly leaves from the green paper for each clothespin. Glue two leaves to one side of each pin; leaf end points should touch and should be centered. Add two or three drops of glue in the area where the leaves touch and sprinkle with glitter. (These form holly berries.)

Attach the garland to a wall or mantle, then evenly space the clothespins and clip them to the garland. Clip one card into each clothespin.

Santa Claus Candle Holder

1 old wine bottle (clean and without labels)
1 taper candle
  Red, white, and black craft paint (other colors
    are optional)
  Large bag of cotton balls
  Glue
  Paint brushes

Paint the lip of the bottle white and the neck of the bottle red. Glue a row of cottonballs along the bottom of the red paint line to put the fur edge on Santa's cap. Stretch two cottonballs and glue them on for eyebrows. With black paint, make two upside-down semicircles for eyes. Below the eyes, paint two tiny upside-down semicircles joined together for a nose. Glue on some cottonballs below the nose to form a mustache. Below the mustache, paint an upright semicircle for the mouth. Leave some room for the face and glue cottonballs all over the rest of the bottle to form Santa's beard and hair. Place a taper candle in the bottle neck.

STOCKING IDENTIFIERS

1 photograph of each family member
4 craft sticks for each photo
   Glue
   Yarn
   Colored markers
   Scissors

Glue four craft sticks together to form a square frame (overlap the ends a little bit). When dry, decorate the frames with colored markers. Tie a length of yarn to each end of the frame tops to form a loop for hanging. Place the frames on top of the photos to check for size. If the photos are too large, trim them to size with the scissors. Glue the photos to the frames and hang them above or beside the stockings.

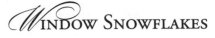WINDOW SNOWFLAKES

3 pipe cleaners
   Faceted beads in assorted sizes
   Monofilament thread

Hold the pipe cleaners in a bundle, then twist them together in the center a couple of times. Spread out the six legs evenly to form a wheel. Thread the beads onto the legs until only about ½ inch is left uncovered. Thread the end partially back into the last bead to form a loop, then flatten the loop to secure the beads. Attach a piece of monofilament for hanging. (These look great on the tree, too!)

Hand Print Wreath

1 paper plate
   Construction paper
   Glue
   Scissors
   Pencil
   Yarn
   Ribbon

Place your hand palm down on a sheet of construction paper (spread fingers and thumb). Trace around it with the pencil and cut out the shape. Place the shape on the edge of the plate and mark its edges lightly with the pencil. Reposition the shape at the last mark, then mark the opposite edge. Continue around the plate in this manner to determine how many hands you'll need to complete the wreath. (If you have some space left over, add one more hand. It's okay to overlap them a bit, and more hands generally make a fuller, prettier wreath.)

Use the shape as a pattern and place it on the paper. Trace around it and cut out the required number of hands. Glue the hands to the edge of the paper plate, then cut away its center. With the ribbon, create a bow and secure to the top center of the paper plate. Glue a loop of yarn to the back of the wreath for hanging.

Note: If you have several children, include all of their handprints in the wreath. Let the children write their names on the appropriate shape.

LOWER POT BELLS

An even number of miniature terra cotta flower pots
1 jingle bell for each pot
1 yard ¼-inch ribbon or rat-tail cording for each pair of pots
Craft paints
Paintbrushes
Holiday decals or stickers (optional)

Paint the pots in holiday colors. Use theme-related designs if you wish, or apply decals or stickers. Set aside.

Gather the lengths of ribbon or cord together in your hand. Pull the ends out from the center a bit so they appear to be different lengths, then fold the bundle cords in half. Tie an overhand knot about two inches from the fold (this forms a loop to hang the bells).

Hold a pot in your hand and thread the cord through the drainage hole, then through the top of a jingle bell. Knot the cord to hold the bell in place. Tie another knot about one inch away from the bell to hold the position of the pot. Repeat the process with each cord end until all the pots and bells are securely fastened. Hang the bells on the front door.

9

GIVING WINTER ITS DUE

THE HOUSE IS DECORATED AND everything looks wonderful. Yule is right around the corner. The essence of the season should be creeping into every part of your being, but something's wrong! You can't quite get into the holiday spirit. The problem is simple: It just doesn't feel like winter. The Sun is shining. It's unseasonably warm. You feel like you should be donning your favorite cutoffs, packing a picnic lunch, and heading for the beach instead of shopping for gifts, deciding on trees, and planning holiday dinners.

Millions of people the world over have this problem. They live in areas where the temperature seldom drops below forty degrees. Marked seasonal change is minimal to nonexistent. Sadly enough, some of them have never even seen ice or snow, much less played in it. So what do they do? How do they get in the mood to celebrate winter—a season that seems imperceptible to their area?

They simply bring winter into their homes.

Bringing winter indoors isn't messy, and it doesn't have to present a problem. All it takes is a little imagination, a few supplies, and a hefty dose of creativity. Regardless of your local climate, the projects below will get you in the mood to celebrate winter and put you on the receiving end of all the joy it brings.

Winter Scene

All you need for this project is a small table, a sturdy piece of styrofoam, and the makings of artificial snow. (Cotton balls, glue, glitter, or white laundry powder work well for this.) If you don't have a table at your disposal, improvise by using what you do have. An undecorated mantle, the top of a bookcase, or a few bare windowsills will do the trick, too.

Start by creating a base from a sheet of styrofoam cut to size. Next, add some snow. This can be done several ways. Some folks like to pull cotton balls apart, glue them to the base, and sprinkle them with a little glitter. Because I like to create hills and valleys, I usually work with a thick paste made from white laundry powder and water. I spread it across the base and add large spoonfuls of the mixture wherever I want to add a hill. Some minimal smoothing with a rubber spatula, a quick sprinkle of glitter, and—presto!—the snowy landscape comes to life.

Now that you have a snow-covered area, take a little time to complete your masterpiece. For your convenience, some favorite ideas are listed below. But don't stop there! Get the whole family in on the act and make use of their ideas and suggestions.

- Add a forest by using evergreen sprigs for trees. Dab some snow paste on the branches with a paintbrush, then sprinkle with glitter.

- Decorate one of the "trees" with sequins, tiny beads, and glitter. Use embroidery floss or thin ribbon for a garland. Place tiny packages beneath it.

- Press a small mirror into the damp mixture for a frozen pond.

- Build a tiny bonfire from small twigs, then glue on red and orange tissue paper scraps for flames.

- Coat two small styrofoam balls with snow paste and press them together for a snowman. Use black adhesive dots for the eyes, nose, and mouth. Braid some heavy yarn together for a scarf and use a doll hat to cover its head.

- Add small houses, miniature people, and tiny toy animals for village and forest scenes.

- For a constant hazy mist, try a bit of dry ice. Just add a few tiny chunks to small containers, then place them in close proximity to the scene.

The possibilities of this project are limitless, but please be warned—once begun, this creation usually takes on a life of its own. One of my friends has been adding to and retouching her original winter wonderland for the last four years. I suspect she'll still be working on it long after I'm old and gray!

BOTTLED SNOWFLAKES

1   white pipecleaner
1   quart jar with a wide mouth
6   tablespoons borax
2   cups boiling water
1   pencil
    Length of twine
    Scissors

Cut the pipe cleaner into three equal lengths, twist them together in the center, then arrange the six legs so they are equidistant from each other. Tie one end of the twine to a leg, and the other end to the middle of the pencil. (For a more ornate flake, tie the twine around the end of each leg in a continuous motion to make a center wheel.) Set aside.

Pour the boiling water into the jar, then add the borax one tablespoon at a time, stirring well to dissolve. (If a little borax settles to the bottom, there's no need to worry, just go on to the next step.) Submerge the pipe cleaner form into the solution, and let the pencil rest on top of the jar.

Leave the snowflake suspended in the solution overnight. The next morning, you'll find it covered with tiny, sparkling crystals. Remove it from the jar, and hang in your window to catch the Sun.

Don't fret if neither of these projects appeals to you. There are lots of other ways you can bring winter into your heart. All it takes is a little imagination. If you're the artistic type, for example, you might experiment with ice carving or shaved ice sculpting, or decorate your windows with a little artificial snow. Another idea might be to give the local ice skating rink a whirl. In lieu of that, surf the travel sections on the Internet for cold weather countries. You'll be thinking snow and ice quicker than you can say, "Happy Yule!"

10

THE YULE TREE

FOR CENTURIES, TREES (OR THEIR PRODUCTS) have played a very important role in winter festivals. It's little wonder, then, that we associate them with the season or that we view them as a holiday icon—even more so than stockings, gifts, or goodies. Fact is, the Yule tree vies with Santa for first place on the Yule menu, and obtaining one usually marks the beginning of the personal holiday for everyone involved. Keeping this in mind, the question of whether or not you will put up a tree probably isn't valid. The question becomes, "What type of tree is most suitable for your lifestyle?"

When I was a child, we were blessed with several hundred wooded acres. For months, Daddy would scout that area for the perfect tree. It had to be just the right size, just the right shape, and have branches just the right length. During that time, Daddy always seemed to be in the woods. Because he was somewhat of a "Greenman" in his own right, I suspect that locating the tree wasn't as difficult a task as he pretended; it just gave him an excuse to be where he felt most comfortable—in the peaceful, quiet solitude of Mother Nature—and far away from Mama's incessant "honey-do" lists. Be that as it may, the perfect tree always arrived just in time for Thanksgiving dinner, and Daddy was the hero of the day.

Daddy passed away some time ago, and his special tree-cutting ritual—a secret rite that no one else shared—died with him. Having cut down a few trees in my time, though, I've developed a few personal techniques—techniques I'm happy to share with folks who wish to obtain their holiday trees in this fashion.

- Spend some time in the woods forming relationships with trees. Talk to them. Listen to them. Befriend them. After you get to know them individually, tell them that you need a Yule tree. See what happens. Chances are that one of them will quickly volunteer.

- When tree-cutting day arrives, gather a piece of rope, a saw with a freshly sharpened blade, and some fertilizer sticks. Talk to the tree and thank it for its gift, then tie the rope around the trunk about six to eight inches above the ground.

- Explain to the tree that you're going to cut its trunk just above the rope. Ask that it move its spirit deep into the ground to avoid injury or pain.

- Make a swift horizontal cut straight through the tree trunk. (I like to use the chain saw for this because it handles the job quickly and effectively.) Thank the tree again, and shove a few fertilizer sticks into the ground close to the trunk base. (This will help new branches sprout and give the tree a headstart on a new beginning.)

- Remember to go back and visit the tree often; take fertilizer sticks with you every three months or so and insert in the ground. It's a very small price to pay for such a wonderful gift.

What if you want a real tree but don't have a personal forest at your disposal? This doesn't have to present a problem, as tree vending stands are abundant and many open as early as a week before Thanksgiving. But is a cut tree the right choice for your family? Several things should be considered before you purchase a real tree. For one thing, they tend to dry out quickly. Because of this, they need to be watered and misted often (two or three times a week, depending upon the humidity levels in your home) to keep them from catching on fire. Another thing to take into consideration is whether you really want to deal with the mess involved. Cut trees tend to shed, and fallen needles can snag carpets and clog vacuum cleaners.

If this doesn't sound like your idea of a good time, you may want to think about an artificial tree, or consider the alternative plan suggested by my friend, Wendy. She and her husband purchase living, potted trees for each of their children. They spend an afternoon talking about Yule while making decorations, listening to holiday music, and decorating the branches. The children keep a tree in their room and care for it during the winter. In the spring, they plant the trees outside. A plaster cast of the childrens' hands and footprints, along with their names and the planting date, rests by each trunk to commemorate the occasion. I can't think of a better way to replenish the Earth and give something back to Mother Nature!

TREE DECORATING

Decorating the tree is perhaps the most looked-forward-to event of the entire Yule-tide season. For one thing, it provides us with a time to do something fun with our families. For another, it gives us a sense of accomplishment. For Pagans, it goes a step further. It gives us an opportunity to unleash our creative energies and make a sort of magic different from any other kind in the cosmos.

No matter what type of tree you use (cut, living, artificial, or other), it's important to bless and consecrate it before you decorate. The blessing doesn't have to be formal or lengthy; simple blessings work just as well. For your convenience, a sample is given below. Use it as a guideline, and expand upon it to suit your purposes. Be creative. Remember that the magic you begin now forms the foundation upon which all personal magic for the coming year is built!

Tree Blessing Ritual

White candle
Pine incense
Salt
Small dish of water
Pet repellent (optional)

Once the tree is placed and ready for decorating, light the incense and the candle. Hold the incense and, beginning in the east, walk around the tree clockwise and chant something like:

> *With Air, I bless this tree of life*
> *And blow away all stress and strife*

Hold the candle and, beginning in the south, walk around the tree and say something like:

> *I bless this tree by warmth of Fire*
> *From which passion flows, and heart's desire*

Hold the water dish and, beginning in the west, walk around the tree and sprinkle it while you say something like:

> *A gift of Water now I give*
> *The cleansing flow by which we live*

Take a handful of salt and, beginning in the north, circle the tree and sprinkle it while you say something like:

> *I give you now the gift of Earth*
> *The grounding force of love and mirth*

Finally, circle the tree once more and say:

> *I cast this loving blessing fast*
> *So peace and good will here shall last*
> *I honor you, my friend, the tree*
> *And bring you thanks now—blessed be*

If you have indoor pets, finish the ritual by spraying the tree liberally with a pet repellent. Both the tree and your pets will be very grateful!

SKIRTING THE TREE

Once the tree is blessed, it's time to decorate, right? Not quite yet. First, it needs a skirt. Decorating a tree without one is a little like trying to accessorize before you put your clothes on; it just doesn't work well. What if you don't have a tree skirt? Not to worry. The suggestions below will solve the problem quickly, easily, and without rummaging around for your favorite headache medication.

TREE SKIRT

      Old newspapers
  2 yards felt (60 inches wide)
      Felt scraps in different colors
      Fusible webbing
      Beads, embroidery floss, trims, and other
         embellishments (optional)
      Yard stick
      Pencil

Unfold three sheets of newspaper and tape them together lengthwise. Measure around the base of the tree. With that measurement, draw a circle of the same size on the upper portion of the newspaper. With the pencil and yardstick, divide the circle into four equal quarters. Extend the lines of one quarter to the length you have in mind for the skirt.

With the yardstick, add ½ inch to each long side of the quarter. Cut out the quarter and pin it to the felt. Cut out the piece. Repeat to cut out three more sections. Sew the sections together using a ½-inch seam allowance, or apply fusible webbing to join them (see package instructions).

Cut out seasonal shapes from the colored scraps and arrange them on the skirt. When you like the way things look, fuse or sew them to the skirt, then embellish as desired.

If you'd like to enchant the new skirt, do it as you place it around the tree. Try something simple like:

Pictured clockwise from top center: Swirled Ornaments, Filled Ornaments, Tree Skirt, Glittered Ornaments.

With you now, I clothe this tree
Bring peace, good will, and harmony
Promote these powers—let them shine
And shower them on me and mine

Now pull out the boxes of ornaments and have a ball. Make a party of it. Laugh, sing, and enjoy the creative flow that bursts forth. That's what magic is all about!

TREE ORNAMENTS

I enjoy making a few new ornaments every year. It not only adds to our collection, but builds memories and magic for Yule celebrations yet to come. Each handcrafted ornament in our household holds its own magic in the form of a spell. Some hold wishes for good health and prosperity. Others, unconditional love and creativity. Still others hold efforts of joy and happiness.

Enchanting an ornament is fun and easy—just state your purpose as you begin to work, and keep that purpose in mind during the creation process. When the ornament is finished, give it a final enchantment by saying something appropriate to its purpose. For example, a simple chant for an ornament designed to promote good health might go something like:

Bring good health to mine and me
As I will, so mote it be

If this appeals to you, pick a purpose and try making some of the ornaments listed below. They're quick, they're easy, and designed to spark the creative spirit in everyone.

*S*WIRLED ORNAMENTS

   Clear plastic or glass ornaments
1 can silver or gold metallic spray paint
1 can white spray paint
1 can spray paint (your choice of color)
1 can clear lacquer spray paint
   Small bucket of water
   Newspapers
1 1-foot length of twine or string for each ornament

Remove the hangers from the ornaments, then thread each ornament cap with a length of twine and knot the ends together to form a loop (the thread will enable you to hang the ornaments to dry). Set aside.

Fill the bucket with about four inches of water. Start at the water's edge and spray some white paint on the water. Continue toward the middle of the bucket, overlap the white, and spray the metallic paint. Overlap the metallic paint, work toward the other edge, and spray the colored paint.

Hold the ornament by the hook and twist it gently into the bucket. (It's important to rotate the ornament; if you dip it, the marbleized effect will be lost.) Remove the ornament and hang to dry. Repeat with the other ornaments.

When ornaments are dry, spray them with clear lacquer. Remove the twine and replace the ornament hangers.

Note: This project gets messy, so you may want to put on some old clothes and spread several thicknesses of newspaper over the work area before you begin. For best results, hang ornaments to dry.

 FILLED ORNAMENTS

Clear glass or plastic ornaments
Your choice of "fillers" (some ideas include potpourri,
   tiny stones or seashells, herbs, holly leaves and
   berries, small cinnamon sticks, ribbons, colored
   embroidery flosses, costume jewelry, confetti, or
   wishes written on slips of colored paper)

Remove the caps from the ornaments, then fill them with your treasures. (Be careful not to add too many fillers—the hanger may not hold the ornament if it is too heavy). Replace caps and hang.

GLITTERED ORNAMENTS

Round glass ornaments
White glue
Gold Glitter
Paper Plate

Remove ornament caps and set aside. Sprinkle a fair amount of glitter on the paper plate. With the glue, draw a pattern on the ornament (you may create your own design or draw suns, stars, holly, or reindeer). Immediately sprinkle with glitter. Shake off excess glitter and hang to dry. When dry, spray with clear lacquer (this prevents glitter from falling off the ornament).

Pictured clockwise from top center: Snow Balls, Garlands, Cinnamon-Apple Ornaments,
Cookie Cutter Ornaments, Herbal/Potpourri Ornaments, Sun-Welcoming Tree Topper.

Herbal/Potpourri Ornaments

Styrofoam balls (bells or other shapes work well, too)
Potpourri or dried herbs
Monofilament fishing line
White glue
1 ½-inch paintbrush
Long needle (dollmaker's needles work well for this)

Cut a piece of monofilament twice the diameter of the ball plus six inches. Fold the line in half, then thread the ends through the needle. Draw the line through the center of the ball so a length hangs from both sides of the ball. Remove the needle and knot the loose ends. Pull the line until it is tight.

With the paintbrush, cover the ball with white glue. Thoroughly coat the ball with herbs or potpourri, let dry, and hang.

Cookie Cutter Ornaments

2 cups flour
1 cup salt
¾–1 cup water
Rolling pin
Cookie cutters
Pencil
Craft paint
Clear acrylic spray
Thread or ribbon

Place the flour and salt in a bowl, then gradually stir in a small amount of water. Continue to add water until the mixture is the consistency of cookie dough. (If you add too much water, don't fret; just mix in a little more flour.) Sprinkle flour on your work surface and roll out the dough to a ½-inch thickness. Cut into shapes with cookie cutters, then with the pencil, poke a small hole in the shape for hanging (make sure the pencil goes all the way through dough). Bake on an ungreased cookie sheet at 250 degrees F until hard and dry—usually about 1 hour. Decorate with paint as desired and spray with clear acrylic. When ornaments are completely dry, thread ribbon through the holes for hanging.

Cinnamon-Apple Ornaments

¾–1 cup apple sauce (depending upon the consistency of sauce)
  1 cup cinnamon
Cookie cutters
Ribbon or yarn
Pencil, ice pick, or knitting needle
Waxed paper

Mix the cinnamon and apple sauce together to make a dough. Roll it out and cut into shapes with cookie cutters. With a pencil, ice pick, or knitting needle, poke a hole in the top for hanging, then place on waxed paper to dry for a day or two. Thread the ribbon or yarn through the hole for hanging.

Snow Balls

Styrofoam balls (any size)
Monofilament or crochet thread
Ivory Snow laundry soap
Silver or white irredescent glitter
Dollmaker's needle
Water
Bowl
Waxed paper
Newspaper
Rubber gloves

With the needle and thread, attach an ornament hanger as instructed in the directions for the Herbal/Potpourri Ornament. Pour some Ivory Snow in the bowl and gradually mix in a small amount of water—about a tablespoon of water at a time—until you have a thick paste. (The mixture should be thick enough to stand in peaks.) Put the ball in the bowl and coat it well with the soap paste. Place on waxed paper and sprinkle with glitter. Hang when dry.

Note: You may want to cover work area with newspaper and use rubber gloves, as this project tends to be messy.

DECORATING WITH GARLANDS

Garlands not only add a finished look to the tree, but because they wrap the tree in one continuous motion, they can also be used as a form of protection. Enchant your garlands by chanting while you work on them. An appropriate chant might go something like:

I string protection into thee
As I work—so mote it be

GARLANDS

Heavy thread (waxed dental floss works well, too)
Sharp needle with a large eye
Cranberries, sunflower seeds, acorns, or prepared popcorn

Since garland creation is just a matter of stringing something together with a needle and thread, no set of instructions is really necessary. One thing you may wish to consider, though, is the length of the thread. Avoid knots and tangles by working in one yard increments. Later, you can knot them together for a one-piece seamless garland.

One of the reasons many folks don't make garlands is because they can't use them again the next year. For magical practitioners, though, that brings an added perk. When the tree comes down, these little goodies can be cut in pieces and hung outside in trees or on fence rails for the birds. It's an ongoing sort of magic, and one that's easily appreciated.

Note: If using sunflower seeds or acorns, soak them in warm water overnight before beginning. This softens the shells and makes piercing easier.

SUN-WELCOMING TREE TOPPER

Large styrofoam ball (4- to 6-inches in diameter)
Several packages of round toothpicks
Gold spray paint
Large dowel stick
Gold glitter (optional)

Begin by poking a hole in the center of the ball with the dowel. Push the dowel in about ¾ of the way through the ball, then remove it. (This hole is the attachment area for the topper.)

Cover the ball with toothpicks. Insert them so approximately ⅔ of each pick protrudes from the outer ball surface. Spray the topper with gold paint. For extra sparkle, sprinkle the topper with glitter while the paint is wet.

11

Holiday Cards

So, the tree and house are decorated, and it's time to kick back, right? Well, maybe for some folks. For me, it signals the time to pull out my holiday card list and get with the program. Today this is something I really enjoy, but in years past, it presented a real problem. Why? While there's nothing difficult about signing, addressing, and stamping cards, finding ones I wanted to send was a major pain. You see, most of the cards in local stores had some sort of Christmas greeting, and because I was Pagan, that just wouldn't do. If your faith or belief system is of something other than Christian origin, it won't do for you, either.

So, what's the solution?

Well, you could do as I did for years and spend several hours picking through boxes of cards. Or you can grab some blank note cards, a dose a creativity, and make your own. Designing the cards doesn't have to be a problem. If you have a computer, there's a good chance that a card design program already exists on the hard drive. It's only a matter of deciding on the message, selecting a picture, and a couple of points and clicks.

If you don't have a computer, there's still no need for worry. Just write your message inside the cards and let your children handle the decorating. It's amazing what kids can do with a few wax crayons or colored markers. Besides, it's an excellent way to save your nerves and stay stress-free. How? By keeping them entertained, you won't have to listen to those "I'm bored" or "It's too nasty to play outside" whines, and with your kids in charge, you'll have a little free time—the time you need to handle all your other holiday duties.

You don't have a computer or kids? Still not a problem. Try holiday stencils and craft paint or involve holiday cookie cutters (trees, stars, and so on). Just trace around them on old sponges with a ballpoint pen and cut them out with scissors. Dampen them with water, dip them in craft paint, and press them lightly onto the front of cards.

Another option is to make snowflake cards. Start with a square piece of paper and fold it in half diagonally to form a triangle. Fold again by bringing the ends of the long edge together. Fold the triangle into thirds by tucking one outer third toward the back and bringing the other toward the front. Snip the two points from the bottom, then cut designs out of the sides. Open the snowflake and glue it onto a solid color card.

If that's too much work to suit your needs, trek down to the local arts and crafts store. They're sure to have a great selection of thematical stickers, rubber stamps, and colored ink. These little items can not only provide a quick fix to your problems, but are quite capable of producing some really beautiful cards—cards that will hold special meaning for you and for all those on your holiday greetings list.

Part III

Gifting, Feasting, and Festing

Solstice Dance

Wrappings and ribbons dance into the room
And step to the lilt of a holiday tune
They splendidly waltz in a colorful swirl
And sing peace and joy as they dip and they twirl

Gifts dance out, too—each one hand-picked with care
They wait for adornment and the time they will share
With those who receive them on this holiday
And anticipate making their lives bright and gay

Then out come the scissors, the tape, and the glue
And name tags, and bells, and the mistletoe, too
A snip here and there, then some ribbon, a bow
Then under the tree all the presents are stowed

To wait for the morning that children all rise
Long before darkness is shed from the skies
To free them with haste from their wrappings and such
And squeal with delight, "Santa! Thank you so much!"

—Dorothy Morrison

12

QUICK AND EASY YULE GIFTS

No matter what type of winter holiday you celebrate, chances are that gift-giving plays a major role. If you're anything like me, you plan to start early but don't quite make it. Of course, that leaves you fighting the crowds at the malls and stores in hopes of finding the perfect gift for everyone. When you're just about done and ready to breathe that sigh of relief, the inevitable happens: You realize that someone's been forgotten and there's little or no time left to rectify the situation. What to do? Try one of the easy gift ideas below.

- Give a gift certificate. These little wonders ensure that recipients will get exactly what they want, and they won't have to stand in long after-holiday exchange lines.

- Have the recipient's natal or numerology chart done. This is a special treat that nearly everyone enjoys. Don't know who handles such things? Try Llewellyn Publications, your favorite New Age store, or check for alternative sources on the Internet.

- Try an aromatherapy kit. These little jewels are easy to obtain in mainstream retail stores all over the country. Best of all, it's something the recipient can use all year long.

- If money is scarce, give a book of personal favor coupons. These could include whatever you like. Some of my personal favorites are a day of housecleaning, a trip to the grocery store, or two hours of errand-running. If you are skilled in Tarot reading, massage therapy, or some other specialty, include those as well.

What if you have to find something really special? Something with a personal touch? Something that says you went out of your way to ensure the recipient's delight? Try working up one of the gifts below. They're fun, they're quick, and most are easy enough for children to make!

Attitude-Changing Pomander

1 orange
1 yard ¼-inch ribbon (color of your choice)
2 boxes whole cloves
    Straight pins
    Pencil

With the pencil, mark a line around the orange from top to bottom and back to top. Use the center of the line as a guide, draw horizontally, and mark another line around the orange. This should give you four equal sections. Place ribbon over the last line drawn, overlap the ends a bit (secure with straight pins), and snip. Use the ribbon to measure the full length of the other line and add approximately fifteen inches. Cut. Fold the ribbon in half and crease well to mark. Use a straight pin to attach the ribbon mark to the bottom of the orange. Work upward and continue to secure the ribbon to the orange with straight pins. Tie the loose ends in a knot.

Use the pointed ends of the cloves to puncture the orange and press cloves into the sections between the ribbons until each section is completely covered. Tie the ribbon ends into a bow. Enchant the pomander by saying something like:

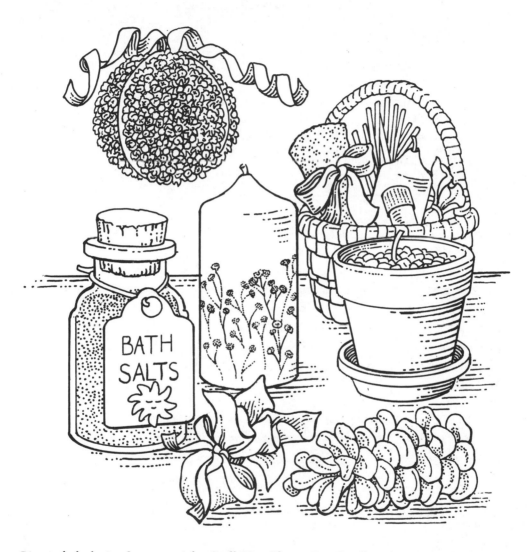

Pictured clockwise from top right: Spell Kits, Flower Pot Candle, Pine Cone Fire Starters, Pressed Herb and Flower Candles, Herbal Energy Sachets, Bath Salts, Attitude-Changing Pomander.

Orange of Sun and heady spice
Keep the closet smelling nice
Bring joy to all who enter there
And keep their outlook bright and fair

Pine Cone Fire Starters

1 pound paraffin
  Cinnamon or gingerbread candle scent
  Candle color (optional)
  Pine cones
  Cooking pot
  Coffee can
  Tongs
  Waxed paper
  Newspapers

Fill the pot ⅓ full of water. Let it warm on medium heat. Place the paraffin in the coffee can and set the can in the pot of water. Leave on stove until the wax melts completely. (While you're waiting for the wax to melt, cover the work area with several thicknesses of newspaper and top off with a sheet of waxed paper.) Remove melted wax from heat and add candle scent.

Use the tongs to dip one pine cone at a time into the wax. With each one, chant something like:

Bring Yule fires up and make them roar
Help birth the Sun and make Him soar
High into the sky at day
To warm our hearts and light our way

Let the excess drain off, then place on waxed paper to harden.

Bath Salts

Zippered plastic bags
Rock salt or Epsom salts
Your choice of essential oil (sunny citrus
   fragrances are nice for Yule)
Food coloring
Bottles or jars with screw-on lids

Fill a zippered bag ¾ full with rock salt. Add the essential oils one drop at a time—it's okay to blend several—until you have a fragrance that you like. Add a few drops of food color, then zip the bag and give it a good shake. If you prefer multi-colored bath salts, add two or three drops of another color, zip the bag, and shake it again. Open the bag and enchant the salts by saying something appropriate to its purpose. In the case of wintergreen salts intended for winter aches and pains, you might chant something like:

> *Bath salts that perfume and smooth*
> *Achy joints and muscles soothe*
> *When mixed in water, bring relief*
> *From aches and pains and minor grief*

Pour into jars or bottles, then cap and label.

Herbal Energy Sachets

4-inch fabric squares in assorted
   colors and patterns
Cinnamon
Allspice
Cloves
Ginger
¼-inch ribbon

In a small bowl, mix the spices until you are pleased with the scent. Place one heaping tablespoon of the mixture in the center of each fabric square. Gather the corners together and secure with a piece of ribbon. Enchant the sachets by saying something like:

Fire of spice and fire of Sun
Put nasty doldrums on the run
Send them packing—do it fast
Bring energy to (name of person) at last

Pressed Herb and Flower Candles

Large pillar candles in your choice of colors
Pressed flowers and herbs appropriate to your magical purpose
    (available at local arts and crafts stores)
2 blocks of paraffin
   1-inch paintbrush
   Waxed paper

Cover the work area with waxed paper, then prepare paraffin as described above for the Yule Pine Cone Starters. Place pressed material onto the candle, dip the brush into the paraffin, and paint over the top. To remove any drips on the candle, dip the brush back into the paraffin, wipe off the excess, and paint over the top.

Enchant the candles while waiting for them to dry. An appropriate chant for a candle designed for increased memory, for example, might go something like:

Memory flow and serve (name of person) well
So data gleaned will stick like gel
Hold information hard and fast
So memory loss is history past

Flower Pot Candle

1 4-inch terra cotta flower pot
1 terra cotta flower pot saucer
1 bag wax potpourri in a scent appropriate to your purpose
1 candle wick and clip (available at arts and crafts stores)

Insert the wick into the drainage hole so the clip is flush with the bottom of the pot. Turn the pot over and set it in the saucer. Hold the wick tautly in the center of the pot, then fill ¾ full with wax cubes. As you fill the pot, chant something appropriate to your magical purpose. For example, a bayberry candle designed to bring money might benefit from a chant such as:

As your perfume floats to and fro
Blow away financial woe
Attract quick cash from near and far
By light of candle, Sun, and star

Trim the wick if necessary.

Spell Kits

1 small basket
1 candle appropriate to magical purpose
1 vial oil appropriate to magical purpose
   A few incense sticks or cones appropriate to magical purpose
   Herbs, stones, and symbols appropriate to magical purpose
   Ribbon in color appropriate to magical purpose
   Paper
   Pen
   Colored cellophane

Arrange the candle, oil, incense, and other items in the basket, then write the spell directions and an appropriate chant on the paper. For instance, a chant for general good fortune might go something like:

Fortuna, Goddess of Fortune and Luck
Cut right through life's crud and muck
Bring good fortune with this spell
Set good luck in motion and let it gel

Roll the paper into a scroll and tie it with a ribbon bow. Wrap the basket in cellophane and secure with ribbon.

Pictured clockwise from top right: Sun Sweatshirt, Flowering Bulb Garden, Scented Mug Coasters, Instant Spa Basket, All-Purpose Incense Kit, Herbal Tea Basket, Potpourri Lamp, Kitchen Wreath.

All-Purpose Incense Kit

1 clean potato chip canister with plastic lid
Wrapping paper with a cosmic theme
   (e.g., moons, stars, or suns)
Glue
Ribbon (optional)
Several dozen sticks of incense
Rubber bands
Small strips of paper

Measure the length and circumference of the canister, then cut a strip of wrapping paper to fit. Wrap the strip around the canister and glue the ends securely. Glue ribbon around the top and bottom if you desire. Gather bundles of similar scented incense sticks together and secure them with rubber bands. Use small pieces of paper to label each type, then attach by slipping the papers under the bands of the appropriate bundles. Replace the lid. Bless the container by saying something like:

> *Please bless these scents, O Mighty Air*
> *That they shall help all magic fare*
> *And bring about the end desired*
> *When they are lit by flame of fire*

Scented Mug Coasters

½ yard printed fabric (45 inches wide)
½ yard quilt batting
Needle and thread
Pinking shears
Dried aromatic herbs (cloves, cinnamon, allspice,
   lavender, or lemon balm are good choices)

With the pinking shears, cut the fabric into six inch squares, then cut one 5½-inch square of quilt batting for each fabric square. Sprinkle about one teaspoon of herbs on top of a batting square and cover it with a second. Baste the two squares together to form a pillow. Place the pillow between two fabric squares (right sides facing out) and pin in place. Stitch the fabric squares together on all four sides (use a ½-inch seam allowance). When the coasters are finished, enchant them by saying something like:

Herbal coasters, do your thing
Harmony, joy, and comfort bring
To all who rest their mugs on you
Make their worries far and few

Herbal Tea Basket

Dried tea herbs of choice (good bets are German chamomile,
    raspberry leaf, lemon balm, peppermint, and combinations
    of rose petals and lavender, and cinnamon and orange peel)
Empty tea bags (available at health food stores)
Tea cup
Small envelopes or plastic zippered bags
1 sheet colored cellophane
Ribbon

First, imbue each herb or herbal combination with the desired properties. When enchanting cinnamon and orange peel, for example, you might say something like:

Orange and cinnamon, when brewed into tea
Grant boundless strength and energy

When all the herbs are enchanted, fill each bag with two or three teaspoons of plant material and fasten shut according to the package directions. Sort the tea varieties into envelopes and label them. Center the tea cup on the cellophane, then arrange the tea bags inside. Gather the cellophane over the cup and tie with a ribbon. Before you deliver the basket, give it a general blessing by chanting something like:

Herbal mixtures—fragrant teas
Grant joy and happiness and ease
To all who drink your powers up
By sipping from the enclosed cup

Kitchen Wreath

Wire ring in desired size
Florist's wire
Cinnamon sticks
Bay leaves
Assorted sprigs of kitchen herbs (rosemary, thyme,
    sage, parsley, lavender, lemon balm, and mint
    are good choices)
Wire cutters
Ribbon
Cookie cutters, measuring spoons, or other kitchen utensils
    (optional)

Gather together three or four sprigs of the same herb, then wind a short length of wire around the stems to secure them. Place the bunch on the ring. Secure another bunch of herbs in the same fashion, place them close to the initial sprigs, then wrap the wire end around the ring. Continue in this fashion until the entire ring is covered. Use small bunches of cinnamon sticks to cover any bare spots, then add cookie cutters, measuring spoons, or other kitchen utensils. Finish off with a ribbon bow.

Note: For better flexibility and working ease, soak dried herb sprigs in cold water for one hour before you begin.

To enchant the wreath, say something like:

O, circle of herbs and kitchen delights
Work your culinary wonders with power and might
Bring your magic to dishes at the cook's invitation
Making each meal that is served cause for real celebration

Instant Spa Basket

2 cups kosher salt
1 cup vegetable oil
3 tablespoons baking soda
3 vitamin E capsules
1 teaspoon dried chamomile
1 teaspoon dried lavender
1 teaspoon dried rosemary
  Jar with screw-on lid
  Loofah pad, bath sponge, or bath puff
  Small basket
  Ribbon
  Colored cellophane

Pulverize the herbs in a food processor or blender, then mix well with the salt and baking soda. Break open the vitamin E capsules and drizzle the oil on top. Add the vegetable oil and stir well while chanting something like:

Herbs and salt, soda and oil
I stir you up to labor and toil
And mix your powers till they're smooth
And winter's dryness you can soothe

Pour the mixture into the jar, tighten the lid, and place it in the basket. Add the loofah, sponge, or puff. Leave a note in the basket for the recipient with the following care instructions, "Apply the mixture to wet, clean skin, scrubbing thoroughly before rinsing." Wrap the basket in cellophane and tie it with a ribbon bow.

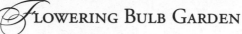LOWERING BULB GARDEN

1   shallow terra cotta flower pot
1   terra cotta pot saucer (same size as pot diameter)
6–7   assorted flowering bulbs
      Potting mix
      Craft paints
      Paintbrushes
      Ribbon (optional)

Paint designs on the pot and the outer edges of the saucer. Some ideas might include Sun/Moon themes, runes, or other magical symbols. Set aside to dry thoroughly.

When the paint is dry, fill the pot with potting mix. Plant the bulbs so the top halves are above ground and they touch each other. Water thoroughly, then tie a ribbon bow around the pot if you like. Deliver with a message that reads something like:

This pot of bulbs heralds the birth of the Sun
The bright days of warmth, light, joy, and pure fun
And as they sprout, so shall the Sun grow
In fullness and strength with a radiant glow
And when He's grown up for all to behold
These bulbs shall then blossom and their petals unfold

OTPOURRI LAMP

1   large jar
1   clear strand of twenty indoor mini-lights
1   6- or 8-inch crocheted doily
      (available at arts and crafts stores)
1   large bag potpourri with red and green accents
      Essential oil of your choice (optional)
      ¼-inch ribbon

Arrange the light strand loosely in the jar so it spirals upward. Fill with potpourri, then add a few drops of essential oil appropriate to your magical purpose. As you add the oil, enchant the lamp contents by saying something like:

Wooden shreds of green and red
Herbs within this lighted bed
Bring (magical purpose) along with light of Sun
As I will, so be it done

Thread the ribbon through the large openings in the doily. (These form a circle and are located about three to four inches away from the doily center.) Place the doily on top of the jar, draw the ribbon tightly around the neck, and tie in a bow.

un Sweatshirt

1 sweatshirt
 Fabric paint and brushes, or indelible marking pen
 Heavy cardboard or foamboard (large enough to stretch
  the shirt so it lays flat during painting and drying)
 Sun transfer

Insert the cardboard into the shirt, and apply the transfer to the shirt front according to package directions. (If you have some artistic ability, you may wish to forgo the transfer and just paint a picture of the Sun instead.) Then paint or write the following beneath the picture.

Welcome to the Newborn Sun
The Shining Light—the Radiant One
Who warms us with His glowing rays
And lights the path of work and play

Pictured clockwise from top center: Crazy Quilt Friendship Egg, Bird Bath, Lacy Amulet Bag, Holiday Dog Collar, Kitty Treats, Dog Biscuits, Peanut Butter Bird Feeder Cakes, Witches' Ladders.

WITCHES' LADDERS

1 yard red satin cord (symbolizes the Mother)
1 yard white satin cord (symbolizes the Maiden)
1 yard black satin cord (symbolizes the Crone)
9 feathers of different colors

Gather the cords together and tie an overhand knot about six inches from the ends. Braid the cords together to invoke the power of the Three-phase Goddess. This is easily done by saying a chant during the braiding process. Try something like:

Maiden, Mother, and Ancient Crone
Your powers to these cords please loan
I ask that You combine them well
And bring Your magic to this spell

Tie another knot when the braiding reaches six inches from the end.

Take a feather and place it in the center of the braid. Knot the cord around it and say an appropriate chant to add the properties of the color to the ladder. For example, when tying a red feather you might say something like:

With this feather, I give you Fire
And love and passion and desire

On the other hand, the chant for a green feather might go something like:

Prosperity, I now bestow
Bring money in and let it flow

You get the idea. The chants don't have to be fancy to be effective. What's important is that you get the point across to the cosmos.

Continue in this manner until all nine feathers are tied into evenly spaced knots. (If you're worried that the feathers will fall out, add a dab of fast-drying glue to each knot.) When all the feathers are secure, enchant the ladder further by saying something like:

Mother, Crone, and Youngest Maid
Carry out the plans I've laid
Add Your blessings to this spell
So it serves (name of person) very well

Lacy Amulet Bag

1 small doily
1 yard ¼-inch ribbon

Thread the ribbon loosely through evenly spaced holes near the outer edge of the doily. Continue past the point where the ribbons meet and thread until you reach a spot opposite the original ribbon entry point. Gently tug on the short end of the ribbon until both sides are the same length. Then pull on both ends to gather the top of the doily and form a bag. Leave the ribbon ends loose, or tie them in a bow to form a bag necklace.

Fill the bag with stones, feathers, shells, or whatever you wish, while chanting something appropriate to your purpose. For example, a bag being charged for general good luck might benefit from a chant like:

The contents that I place in here
Shall draw good luck from far and near
And mingled together, shall increase in power
And gain new strength with every hour

Crazy Quilt Friendship Egg

1 plastic egg container (the kind from pantyhose works well)
1 sharp nail (large)
   Assortment of thin fabric scraps, braids, laces, and trims
   Fabric glue
¼ yard ribbon
   Cigarette lighter
   Scissors

Pull the egg apart. Heat the pointed end of the nail with the lighter (be careful not to burn yourself). Push the nail point through the top of the egg to form a hole. Glue fabric scraps onto both container halves; overlap fabric shapes as you go until the pieces are completely covered. Glue braid, trim, or lace over fabric seams. Allow to dry thoroughly, then with the nail point, puncture the fabric over the hole. Fold the ribbon in half, hold both ends together, and tie a knot about 3 inches from the ends. Draw the ribbon ends through the hole and tie a knot inside the top half to secure. Fill the egg with sachets, small bags of bath salts, or other small gifts. Then attach a note that reads something like:

Eggs symbolize life, with no beginning or end
Like the life that we share in our circle of friends
I give you this egg with its gift and my love
And blessings that flow from the cosmos above
When it's empty, refill with a gift for a friend
So the circle grows onward without any end

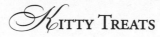itty Treats

Small amount of dried catnip (1 tablespoon for each treat)
Sewing thread
4-inch fabric square (one for each treat)
Ribbon

Place a tablespoon of catnip in the center of the fabric. Gather the ends together (leave a two-inch tail), and wind the thread tightly around the pouch to secure the catnip. Tie off the thread using a double knot and cut the ends close to the wrapping. Place the ribbon over the thread wrapping and tie it in a bow.

Note: To prevent choking, burn ends of ribbon; you may also want to supervise cats while they play.

Enchant the kitty treat by saying something like:

Goddess Bast of feline friends
Your powers to this treat, please lend
I ask You now to bless this toy
And fill it full of kitty joy

eanut Butter Bird Feeder Cakes

(Use like suet cakes for the bird feeder)

Wild bird seed
Large jar of peanut butter
Waxed paper
Cellophane wrap

Remove the lid from the peanut butter, then place the jar in the microwave. Heat on high at 30 second intervals until the peanut butter is runny. Pour it into the bowl and add enough bird seed to make a thick, stiff paste.

Turn out the paste onto waxed paper and, with your fingers, roll the mixture into a log. Wrap the log in waxed paper and put it in the freezer for one to two hours. Just before delivery, slice the log and wrap individual slices in cellophane. Enchant the cakes by saying something like:

In snow and ice, in rain and sleet
Bring hungry birds a festive treat
Let them flock and keep them fed
In bitter cold and Winter dread

Holiday Dog Collar

Nylon or fabric collar
Small jingle bells
Sprigs of artificial holly (optional)
Fabric paint
Paint brush
Hot glue

Paint the pet's name on the collar (evenly centered), and allow to dry. Glue on the bells and add some artificial holly if you like. Enchant the gift by saying something like:

Diana, Goddess of Canine Friends
Bless this gift and Your ear bend
To listen as these small bells ring
And watch (name of dog) while wandering
And keep him/her safe and quite secure
So no hardships this pet endures
Please always bring him/her safely home
No matter how far (name of dog) should roam

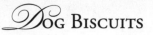og Biscuits

3 cups whole wheat flour
½ cup powdered milk
1 egg
1 cube chicken, liver, or beef bouillon
¾ cup water
⅓ cup margarine
¼ teaspoon salt

Place water, bouillon, and margarine in a large bowl; microwave on high for one minute. Stir in all other ingredients, and add the flour last. Dough will be stiff. Roll out to ½-inch thick on a lightly floured surface. Cut into shapes with cookie cutters. Place on a greased cookie sheet and bake at 325 degrees F for 35 to 40 minutes (biscuits should be hard). Turn off heat and leave in the oven for one hour.

IRD BATH

3 large terra cotta flower pots (purchase the largest pot
     you can find, the next smallest size, and the next;
     stack them before purchasing to ensure they all
     fit together)
1 terra cotta saucer to fit the largest pot
     Various shades of spray enamel or other
      water-based paint
     Clear spray enamel
     Clear silicone sealer
     Acrylic paints in various colors (optional)
     Paint brushes (optional)

Give the pots several coats of colored spray enamel or paint. (Although you can paint them all the same color if you wish, painting each piece a different color gives the finished product a very festive look.) Paint the saucer inside and out, giving an extra coat to the inner surface. When dry, turn the largest pot upside down so the bottom is facing up. Squeeze a thick coat of silicone sealer around the pot about one inch from the upper edge. Turn the next largest pot upside down and place it on top of the other. Apply the sealer, then turn the last pot upside down and place it on top. Spread a heavy coat of silicone sealer to the top of the last pot. Center the saucer (right side up) and press it firmly onto the coated area. Let dry for at least twenty-four hours, then using acrylic paints, add symbols or pictures if you like. Finish with two coats of clear spray.

Note: Bring the bath indoors during cold weather, as the cold could harm the exterior.

To enchant the bird bath, try chanting something like:

O little pots of earthenware
Now a bath for birds to share
Bring pure delight to feathered friends
And call them from the Earth's four ends
So they may frolic and have fun
In splashing water, 'neath the Sun

13

WRAPPING UP THE SEASON

YOU NOW HAVE THE PERFECT gift for everyone on your list. All you have to do is wrap it up. Before you get out the ribbon and wrapping paper and tape, give some thought to the end result. It would be a pity for the perfect gift to look just like any other. It needs to look special—as special as the gift itself—so special, in fact, that the recipient can't wait to open it. The perfect gift does, after all, deserve the perfect packaging.

Just how much can you do with wrapping paper and ribbon? More than you might imagine! You only have to look at it from the right perspective: Once you view the process as "clothing" the gift rather than just wrapping it, you'll start to see things in a whole new light. The tips on the following pages will get you started.

Fun Wrap Ideas

- Try a basket for a small assortment of related gifts. Wrap in colored tissue or cellophane and secure with ribbon.

- Old Valentine's candy boxes are also good bets for gift assortments. Use craft or fabric paint to change the boxes to green. Cut a snowflake design from a paper doily and use it for a name tag.

- Wrap kitchen gifts in dishcloths or towels. Secure the ends with pot scrubber (the type with the hole in the middle), thread them through a ring of measuring spoons, or clip them together with an assortment of colored clothespins.

- Decorative hand towels, fingertip towels, and washcloths make great gift dressings for bath and boudoir gifts; just secure the ends with matching satin ribbon.

- Instead of paper, try velvet, taffeta, silk, or another rich fabric in a solid color. Wrap again with a length of lace, then tie with a velvet ribbon.

- Substitute newspaper for gift wrap, then tie with heavy red yarn or ribbon. Use a white notecard for the name tag and mark it with bold black letters.

- Brown paper (leftover grocery bags work well for this) also makes an attractive wrap. Tie with twine, and hot glue small pine cones, holly, and fir snippets to the center. Secure four or five cinnamon sticks together with red or green yarn and use for a bow.

- Use solid color wrapping paper and tie with raffia. Attach a couple of candy canes or a decorated cookie to the center of the bow.

- Cut a shape out of an old sponge, dip it in craft paint, and use to decorate plain white or brown paper.

- Spruce up solid color packages by gluing on individual foil-wrapped candies. Chocolate bells or candies with Santa faces are good choices.

GREAT NAME TAG IDEAS

- Attach small tree ornaments to ribbon ties, then write the name on one of them using an indelible marker.

- Bake a large cookie and attach it to the package with a bit of icing. "Write" the name with chocolate chips, cinnamon candies, sprinkles, or icing.

- Holiday cookie cutters make attractive name tags, too. Just use an indelible marker to add the name.

14

Let's Party!

As with choosing the perfect gift, festive Yuletide parties don't just come together overnight. There are guest lists to ponder, menus to create, and battles to be won in supermarket checkout lines. Even more important, you need to ensure that all of your guests have a wonderful time. The best way to do that, of course, is to create the proper atmosphere.

Isn't the fact that you've already decorated the house and tree enough? No! While those decorations announce that you're aware of the holiday season in progress, they don't say, "Party!" In order to get that cheerful word to issue forth, you have to do something more, and nothing gets a celebratory mood going quicker than a lavishly set holiday table.

Lavish doesn't have to mean expensive. There's no need to get out grandma's good lace tablecloth or invest in china, crystal, or sterling silver flatware. In fact, you probably have almost everything you need right at home, and if you don't, you can find any missing items at the five-and-dime. The idea here is to create a fun and festive atmosphere, one that will transport your guests into a magical holiday wonderland—a wonderland that they'll remember for years to come. Ideas and instructions follow below.

Holiday Tablecloth

1 sheet or piece of fabric (large enough to
    cover the table)
Stencils in a holiday theme
Fabric paints
Paint brushes or old sponges
Masking tape

Wash, dry, and iron the sheet. (It's very important that it be free of wrinkles before you begin painting.) Lay the stencils on the fabric, then use masking tape to secure. Apply paint with brushes or sponges. If you want to use the same design somewhere else on the cloth, carefully lift the stencil from its current position, tape it securely to the desired area, and dab in more paint. Care for the tablecloth according to the instructions on the back of the paint container.

Party Placemats

1 15-by-24-inch length of felt for each placemat
    (or purchase pre-made placemats)
2 15-by-24-inch lengths of clear contact paper
    for each placemat
Felt scraps in assorted colors
Fabric glue
Scissors

Cut holiday shapes (e.g., bells, stars, trees, wreaths, or snowflakes) from the scraps, then glue them to the placemats. Carefully peel the backing from one sheet of contact paper and lay it over the arrangement; be sure to work out all creases and air bubbles. Add a sheet of contact paper to the other side as well. Repeat the process for each placemat. (For other placemat ideas, see chapter 8.)

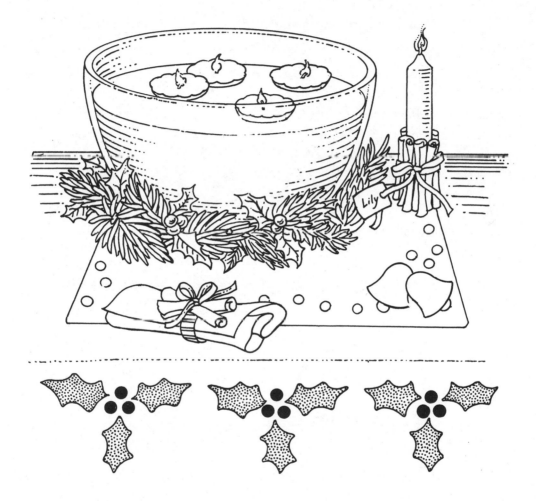

Pictured clockwise from top: Floating Holiday Centerpiece, Place Cards, Party Placemats, Holiday Tablecloth, Napkin Rings.

Napkin Rings

1   2-by-5-inch strip of posterboard for each ring
    Foil gift wrap (or aluminum foil)
    Adhesive tape
    Evergreen sprigs, cinnamon sticks, or small tree ornaments
    Ribbon
    Hole punch
    Glue (optional)

Cover each cardboard strip with gift wrap and secure with adhesive tape. (An easy way to cover the strip is to wrap it just like you would a package.) Bring the two ends together, overlap them a bit to form a ring, and secure them with tape. Punch a hole on each side of the seam, then thread the ribbon through the holes so the loose ends are on top of the ring. Arrange the sprigs, cinnamon sticks, or ornaments on top of the seam. Secure with glue if necessary. Double-knot the ribbon around the decoration, then tie the ends into a bow.

Place Cards

Small white cards (unlined 3-by-5-inch index cards
    cut in half work well)
Small pillar candles (approximately 6-by-½-inches)
Small candy canes or cinnamon sticks
Hot glue
Ribbon
Hole punch
Pen

Write the name of each guest on a card, punch a hole in upper left-hand corner, then put aside. Glue cinnamon sticks or candy canes vertically side by side around the outside of the candle until it's completely covered. (If working with candy canes, place the "hooks" at the bottom edge of the candle facing out. This gives the candle a stable base.) Tie a piece of ribbon securely around the outside of the candle. Thread both ends through the hole in the place card and tie with a bow. Send these home with your guests as a memento of the occasion.

FLOATING HOLIDAY CENTERPIECE

Odd number of floating candles
Small punch bowl
Assorted seasonal greenery
Water
Sequin confetti (optional)

Fill the bowl ¾ full of water. Add the candles and the sequins. Arrange the greenery around the base of the bowl. (For other centerpiece ideas, see the Quick and Easy Yule Decorations section.) As you light the candles for the first time, chant something like:

Flame of fire, burning bright
Warm our spirits with your light
Urge the Sun to shine with Thee
As I will, so mote it be

Just before your guests arrive, bless everything on the table by saying something like:

Ancient Ones of Holiday Cheer
Bring Your jovial spirit to all who sit here
Bless these items with joy and happiness, too
And lend good fun tonight in all that we do

15

PARTY IDEAS AND GAMES

PARTIES—ESPECIALLY THOSE AT YULE—allow us to feel like kids again. That's why we enjoy them so much. But sometimes, parties get off to a slow start and the event is half over before things really get rolling. To prevent this from happening to your party, try a few of the tips below. I've also included some great icebreakers and party game ideas. They're guaranteed to bring out the child in even the most stuffy of fuddy-duddies. (Don't forget to give small prizes to the winners!)

SIMPLE PARTY IDEAS

- Plan the guest list carefully; only invite folks who share some common interests. That way, no one will be left out in the cold with nothing to talk about.

- Make sure you introduce your guests to each other. Nothing makes a party fall flat more quickly than when guests don't know each other.

- Leave a few things to do in the kitchen after the guests arrive. It gives you an opportunity to rescue any partygoer that seems to be floundering.

- Play seasonal music. Few can resist the urge to sing or whistle along—and once the music summons their voices, shyness becomes a thing of the past.

- For a real twist, take a tip from ancient festival celebrants. Encourage your guests to arrive in costume and take on the persona of the character they portray.

- Don't forget the aromatherapy factor. Put on a pot of simmering holiday potpourri made from cloves, allspice, nutmeg, cinnamon, and apple and orange peel. It's guaranteed to fill every guest on your list with the holiday spirit.

GAMES

Holiday Charades: Only allow holiday-related phrases. Carol titles, holiday movies, and phrases like "sugar-plum fairy" are great game starters.

The Apple Roll Race: Pair your guests into teams and give each team an old pair of pantyhose with an apple in one foot. Have one member of each team tie the hose around their waist, then place an unbreakable ornament or styrofoam ball in front of them. Ask the other team members to stand on the other side of the room. The object of the game is to move the ornament across the room to the respective team member with only the aid of the apple. The first team to accomplish this task wins.

Ye of a Thousand Words: Hand out pencils and sheets of paper with different holiday words or phrases on them. Words like Winter Solstice, Christmas, Hanukkah, Holiday Tree, or Mistletoe are good choices. Have guests see how many words they can make from the letters written on their sheets.

Conversation Continuity: Toss slips of paper marked with holiday words into a bag or hat. Pass the container around so each person can draw out a slip. The first person must make a statement that ends with the word on their slip. The next person must begin a statement with the previous person's last word, and end the statement with the word they hold their hand.

Holiday Word Search: Although the word search below was written with children in mind, adults will enjoy this game, too. Give a prize to the first person to find all the words.

```
F  W  T  C  E  C  H  A  P  P  I  N  Q  K  W  A  W
A  R  N  M  I  N  C  A  P  P  H  T  A  S  P  I  S
A  E  C  M  I  N  C  E  M  E  A  T  L  G  N  C  O
T  A  E  M  G  L  I  L  G  S  N  S  M  T  A  A  L
B  T  S  O  I  M  N  W  Q  Y  U  L  E  W  O  N  S
P  H  O  L  F  S  O  H  L  E  K  R  R  S  A  D  T
T  R  E  E  T  K  T  O  A  B  K  Z  R  I  F  Y  I
S  A  T  U  R  N  A  L  I  A  A  W  Y  V  Q  C  C
C  A  D  S  B  E  L  L  E  M  H  B  X  S  Q  A  E
V  N  S  Q  N  J  Y  U  T  L  W  M  U  C  N  Z
H  J  L  T  Z  W  L  T  H  S  O  C  A  N  D  E  E
I  V  Y  V  A  E  A  D  D  T  S  E  S  X  S  W  C
D  E  S  T  S  N  B  R  T  H  E  T  Z  S  A  D  V
Y  T  R  N  S  W  D  A  G  G  M  E  N  O  R  A  H
P  O  I  N  S  E  T  T  I  A  Q  D  A  T  D  R  H
C  T  E  V  R  E  W  S  S  L  E  T  W  S  C  K  E
P  O  S  I  T  I  S  E  T  W  E  L  D  N  A  C  Y
```

Bell	**Gift**	**Menorah**	**Santa**	**Tinsel**
Candle	**Hanukkah**	**Merry Xmas**	**Saturnalia**	**Tree**
Candy Cane	**Holly**	**Mincemeat**	**Snow**	**Winter**
Dark	**Ivy**	**Mistletoe**	**Solstice**	**Wreath**
Fir	**Light**	**Poinsettia**	**Sun**	**Yule**

16

Eat, Drink, and Be Merry

There's nothing like the holidays to bring out the culinary magician in everybody. Magically speaking, it unblocks the creative flow and allows the forces of inspiration to surge again, but the mundane reasons are just as important. It gives us an excuse to prepare special dishes, rich foods, and other delightful items that we wouldn't serve on a regular basis, and in this time of reduced fat, low sodium, and health consciousness, it also gives us an excuse to eat them!

That having been said, the recipes offered on the following pages obviously do not reflect a balanced diet. Rather, most of them are culinary delights designed to spark your creativity, add a special sense of celebration to the holidays, and curb those incessant cravings rendered by the sweet tooth. So go ahead and give them a whirl. Your tastebuds will thank you, and so will your family.

Yuletide Sweets

Decorated Yule Cookies

What would a winter holiday be without decorated sugar cookies? Cut them out in traditional shapes such as trees, Santas, or reindeer; for a real Pagan celebration, don't forget to add the Sun to your cookie cutter list. Save some of these for the Yule tree, too. With a quick spritzing of spray-on craft lacquer, they also make excellent tree decorations!

¾ cup (1½ sticks) butter, softened
1 cup sugar
1 egg
1 teaspoon vanilla extract
2 cups flour
2 teaspoons baking powder
½ teaspoon salt
Colored sugars, decorative candies, sprinkles, or frosting

Mix the butter and sugar together until creamy, then beat in the egg and vanilla. Add the dry ingredients and mix well. Cover dough and refrigerate for 2 hours.

Preheat oven to 375 degrees. Roll out dough to ⅛-inch thick and cut out shapes with cookie cutters. Decorate as desired using colored sugars, decorative candies, sprinkles, or frosting. Place on cookie sheet and bake for 8 to 10 minutes.

Makes 30 to 40 cookies depending upon size of cookie cutter

Gingerbread Cookies
(French/German)

When it comes to the holiday season, nothing can put you in the spirit more quickly than the delicious aroma of freshly baked gingerbread. Originally prepared at Easter as well, it has now become a winter holiday staple. (For more information about its history and significance, see chapter 2.)

½ teaspoon ground ginger
½ teaspoon ground cloves
¼ teaspoon nutmeg
1 teaspoon cinnamon
1 teaspoon baking soda
½ cup brown sugar
¾ cup molasses
½ teaspoon salt
¾ cup (1½ sticks) butter
1 egg, beaten
3⅓ cups all-purpose flour

Place ginger, cloves, nutmeg, cinnamon, sugar, molasses, and salt in the top of a large double boiler (with water on the bottom). On medium-high heat, stir constantly until the mixture comes to a boil. Remove from heat and stir in butter. Once butter melts completely, add the egg and mix well. Stir in the flour and baking soda. Chill dough in refrigerator for three hours.

Preheat oven to 350 degrees. Roll out dough to a ¼-inch thickness on lightly floured surface. Cut out shapes with cookie cutters. (If using cookies for tree decorations, make a hole in the top of the cookie with a large pointed object so a hanger can be inserted easily.) Bake for 12 to 15 minutes. Edges should be slightly brown. Decorate with icing if desired.

Makes 30 to 40 cookies depending upon size of cookie cutter

Miz Sadie's Pecan Divinity

Miz Sadie's Pecan Divinity has always been one of my holiday favorites. I used to think it was only traditional in the South, but after living in many areas of the country, I've discovered that Americans everywhere enjoy its scrumptious goodness during the Yuletide season.

- 2⅔ cups sugar
- ⅔ cup light corn syrup
- ⅔ cup water
- 2 egg whites
- 1 cup chopped pecans

Place sugar, corn syrup, and water in a saucepan. Stir constantly over medium heat until the mixture reaches the hard crack stage. (To check, let a drop fall into ice water. It's ready when it forms hard threads.) Beat the egg whites until they stand in peaks. Beating constantly, pour the hot mixture in a thin stream into the egg whites. Fold in the pecans, and continue to mix until thick. From a buttered spoon, drop by teaspoonfuls onto waxed paper. Store in an airtight container.

Makes 35 to 40 pieces

Quick Ambrosia

This heavenly dessert has been a seasonal tradition in my family for at least four generations. It's so rich and delectable, I can't imagine having a Yuletide celebration without it!

- 1 15-ounce can fruit cocktail
- 1 11-ounce can mandarin oranges
- 1 cup chopped walnuts
- ½ cup shredded coconut
- 12 ounces sour cream (use fat-free, light, or regular)

Drain the fruit cocktail and oranges, then mix all the ingredients together in a large bowl. Voilá! A delicacy fit for the gods! Chill before serving.

Serves 8

Mama's Mock Mincemeat Pie
(British)

An ancient British holiday tradition, this pie was originally served as an entrée. The reason for this was that the main ingredient in the filling was diced lamb; thus the name Mincemeat Pie. The meat was removed from the ingredient list years ago, and though you can find something called mincemeat in most modern supermarkets, it's expensive and contains no animal products. The recipe below, however, doesn't require mincemeat and produces a terrific dessert at a reasonable price.

2   pre-prepared pie crust rounds*
2   cups peeled and chopped baking apples
1   cup raisins
1   cup brown sugar
⅛   teaspoon cinnamon
⅛   teaspoon nutmeg
⅛   teaspoon salt
1   cup sour cream

Preheat oven to 450 degrees. Line a 9-inch pie pan with one crust round and set aside. Combine all other ingredients, mix well, and pour into pie pan. Place the second crust on top, seal the edges, cut patterns on top crust (so steam escapes), and sprinkle with cinnamon sugar. Bake for 10 minutes. Reduce oven temperature to 350 degrees and bake for an additional 45 minutes. Remove from oven and serve.

Note: You may want to place pie on a baking sheet to catch drips, and put narrow pieces of tin foil around the outside edge of crust to prevent it from burning. Remove foil during last ten minutes of baking.

*Piecrust rounds are easily found in the supermarket dairy case. They taste great and are real time-savers.

Serves 6

Yule Log

(French)

If you've never made a Yule Log Roll before, now is the time to give it a shot. Contributed by Su Walker, this Yule Log recipe will not only look lovely on your festival table, but is so simple and delicious that you'll be marking off the days until you can make it again!

¼ cup butter or margarine
1 cup chopped walnuts or pecans (or a mixture of both)
1 cup flaked coconut
1 14-ounce can sweetened condensed milk
4 eggs
½ cup water
1 box chocolate cake mix (or homemade cake from scratch)
1 cup powdered sugar
1 can ready-to-spread chocolate frosting (or your own homemade frosting)
   Green gummy candies and red hot cinnamon candies
   Small Yule candles (optional)

Preheat oven to 350 degrees. Line a 15 x 10 inch jelly roll pan with aluminum foil; make sure that the foil lines the sides and bottom completely. Melt butter in the foil-lined pan (I pop it in the oven and watch it carefully, then remove it when all is melted), sprinkle evenly with nuts and coconut, and drizzle the condensed milk on top.

In a large bowl, beat the eggs at high speed for 4 to 6 minutes or until thick and lemon colored. At very low speed, gradually blend in water. Add the cake mix and blend for a minute or so more until all the dry ingredients are mixed. Pour this batter over the condensed milk and spread it out evenly. Bake at 350 degrees for 30 to 35 minutes or until the top springs back when touched lightly in the center.

Lightly sprinkle a large kitchen towel with powdered sugar. Remove the cake from the oven, cover it with the sugared side of the towel, and immediately turn the cake upside down onto the towel.

Remove the foil carefully; try not to disturb the hot filling on top. Begin with one of the short sides of the cake and gently roll up with the filling inside the roll. When you've rolled up the entire cake, wrap the towel around it and let it cool completely.

Ice with the chocolate frosting, then comb a fork through the frosting to fashion tree bark. Garnish with green gummy candies trimmed to look like holly leaves and use the cinnamon candies for holly berries. Add Yule candles if you like.

Makes 8 to 10 servings

Solar Candy

(German)

Originally used to decorate holiday trees, these candied delights serve to remind us that the Sun (citrus fruit) is always born through ice and snow (symbolized by the granulated sugar coating).

        Rind from 3 oranges
        Rind from 3 lemons
        Rind from 1 grapefruit
1¼ cups honey
 1   cup water
 1   teaspoons ginger
 ½   teaspoon cinnamon
        Sugar

With a sharp knife, remove as much of the inner white matter as possible from the rinds, then cut them into bite sized pieces and place them in a pot of water. Bring the pot to a rolling boil, then reduce the heat and allow to simmer for 5 minutes. Drain the rinds and add fresh water to the pot, then repeat the boil/simmer/drain process four more times. After the final draining, add 1 cup of water, the honey, and the spices to the pot. Stir the mixture well, then add the rinds. Cook the mixture over low heat until the rinds are tender. Sprinkle waxed paper with sugar, place the rinds on top, then sprinkle with sugar again. Allow candy to air dry for several hours. When completely dry, store in an airtight container.

Makes 50 to 60 pieces depending upon fruit size

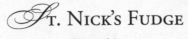t. Nick's Fudge
(Dutch)

Although fudge is popular in many countries during the holiday season, it seems to have a special significance in Holland on December 6, St. Nicholas' Eve. This fudge recipe is quicker and easier to make than most, and the end result is absolutely yummy!

16   squares (2 packages) semisweet chocolate
 1   14-ounce can sweetened condensed milk
 2   teaspoons vanilla extract
 1   cup chopped walnuts

Place chocolate and sweetened condensed milk in a microwave-safe bowl and heat in the microwave for 3 minutes on high, stirring once halfway between heating time. Remove from microwave and stir until chocolate is completely melted. Stir in the vanilla and nuts. Spread in a heavily buttered or foil-lined 8-inch pan. Place in refrigerator until the candy hardens, then cut into squares.

Makes 25 pieces

Cherry Cola Salad

This dessert salad is yet another personal Yuletide favorite. For an extra touch of festivity, use lime gelatin and pour it into a holiday tree mold, garnish it with fresh mint leaves or sprigs of rosemary, and use it as a dinner centerpiece.

 2   small packets cherry gelatin
 1   16-ounce can bing cherries
 1   8-ounce can crushed pineapple
    Cola-flavored soda
16   ounces cream cheese cut into small chunks
 1   cup chopped pecans or walnuts

Empty the gelatin into a pot. Do not add water. Drain the cherries and pour the juice into a large measuring cup. (This liquid will make up part of the gelatin water requirement.) Check the package directions for water amounts, then add enough cola to the cherry juice to make up the rest of the measurement. Add the mixture to the gelatin and prepare as directed. Gradually add the pieces of cream cheese, mixing well until they are partially blended with the gelatin mixture. Add the pineapple, cherries, and nuts. Pour the hot gelatin mixture into a pan or mold. Place in the refrigerator and allow to chill until firm.

Serves 8

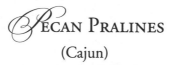

Pecan Pralines

(Cajun)

For most folks, it's impossible to grow up in Texas without having a dab of Cajun heritage spilling over onto the personal root system. I picked up more than most, though, for my mother's early environment included the luxury of a Cajun cook. That being the case, Mama learned to make these rich candies early on, adding a touch of bourbon for a special holiday treat.

3 cups sugar
5 tablespoons light corn syrup
1 5-ounce can evaporated milk
1 teaspoon baking soda
3 cups pecan halves
4 tablespoons bourbon

Mix sugar, corn syrup, and evaporated milk in a large saucepan. Stirring constantly, heat to a rolling boil. Remove from stove, add baking soda, and let foam. Add pecan halves, continuing to stir constantly, and return to heat until the mixture reaches an amber color. Remove from stove and add bourbon. Beat by hand until smooth and glossy (about 2 minutes). Drop by tablespoonfuls onto foil or waxed paper. Store in an airtight container when cool.

Makes 25 to 30 pralines

Yule Log Roll
(French)

This is a richer alternative to the previous Yule Log recipe. Contributed by Ina Rae Ussack, this Yule Log Roll is a little more time-consuming to make, but the results are well worth the effort!

¾ cup flour
1 cup sugar
3 eggs
⅔ cup strawberry jam or cranberry relish
1 teaspoon baking soda
½ teaspoon salt
½ cup powdered sugar
¾ cup walnuts
1 can chocolate frosting

Filling
8 ounces cream cheese
1 cup powdered sugar
2 tablespoons butter
1 cup walnut pieces
1 teaspoon vanilla extract

Preheat the oven to 350 degrees. Grease a jelly roll pan and line it with waxed paper. In a medium mixing bowl, beat eggs and sugar until well blended. Add the jam or relish and beat well, then add flour, soda, and salt. Pour into prepared pan. Sprinkle the walnuts on top. Bake for 15 minutes or until cake springs back when lightly touched. Immediately loosen sides of the cake from the pan. Sprinkle the powdered sugar on a towel, then turn out the cake on top. Roll up the towel and cake, starting with the short end of the cake. Let cool on a wire rack, then mix the filling. Unroll the cooled cake and spread the filling on top, leaving a 1-inch border around the edges. Roll the cake tightly as for a jelly roll, then wrap it in foil and place it in the refrigerator. Ice with chocolate frosting just before serving.

Makes 8 to 10 servings

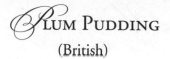LUM PUDDING
(British)

A modern variation of the recipe popular in seventeenth century England, plum pudding must age and should be prepared at least four weeks in advance of serving. For a real treat, try stirring in the traditional portent charms (for information, see chapter 2). Once you do, your family will look forward to eating this dish every year!

1 cup milk
1 cup molasses
1 cup raisins
1 cup ground suet
3 cups flour
1 teaspoon baking soda
1 teaspoon cinnamon
½ teaspoon ground clove
¼ teaspoon nutmeg
1 teaspoon salt

Mix all ingredients together thoroughly, pour the mixture into the well-greased top of a double-boiler, and cover with foil. Fill the boiler bottom half full with water, then set the mixture pan on top. Let simmer for 3 hours; add water when necessary. Let cool, remove from pan, wrap in foil, and store in the refrigerator or freezer.

Serves 10 to 12

 Dragon's Layer Cake

(Irish)

Contributed by Jacquie Brennan, this rich, luscious cake is not only scrumptious, but quick and easy to make. Since the dragon has long represented fire in the Earth while Winter Solstice marks the return of its warmth, this great dessert also provides the perfect symbolism for your Yuletide celebration.

  6 ounces best quality dark chocolate (60 percent
      or more cocoa solids)
     Grated zest of 1 orange
  ½ cup (1 stick) sweet butter, at room temperature
1½ cups confectioners' sugar
     Juice of 2 oranges
  ¼ cup Cointreau, Grand Marnier, or cognac (or to taste)
30 sponge fingers (Savoy biscuits)
     A large oblong serving plate

DECORATION
1¼ cups heavy cream, whipped to soft peaks
  ¼ cup Cointreau, Grand Marnier, or cognac (or to taste)
  1 ounce grated curls of best dark chocolate

Melt the chocolate, broken into pieces, in a heatproof basin over a pan of boiling water. Grate the zest from the orange. Cream the butter until very light in a large mixing bowl. Add the (slightly cooled) melted chocolate and the grated orange zest and combine well. Sift the confectioners' sugar over the top and mix in well. Combine the juice of the 2 oranges with the Cointreau or other liqueur in a separate bowl. One at a time, quickly dip each end of the sponge fingers into the liquid and lay the first 10 fingers side by side in a row on the serving plate. Top the sponge fingers with about ¼ of the chocolate icing mixture and spread evenly. Follow by adding two more layers each of 10 dipped fingers with chocolate mix in between and finish by covering the whole with the remaining chocolate icing. Smooth with a palette knife dipped in hot water. Leave to set firm in the refrigerator for about 2 hours.

For the decoration, firmly whip the cream and add the liqueur. Spread lightly on cake and generously sprinkle with grated dark chocolate curls, fine slivers of orange zest, or both!

Makes 10 generous servings

CRESCENT CAKES
(Celtic)

Although more like a cookie than a cake, these are the perfect little treats to serve at Yule rituals of every type. For a real boost of magical power, invoke the spirit of Yule by chanting the names of your favorite Deities while you gather the ingredients. You'll be amazed at the results!

1½ cups flour
1 cup confectioners' sugar
1 cup ground almonds
3 drops almond extract
1 teaspoon vanilla extract
½ cup softened butter
1 egg yolk
2 tablespoons honey

Combine the first five ingredients in a large bowl, then add the butter, egg yolk, and honey. Mix well. Cover and place in the refrigerator for 2 hours. Remove the dough, pinch off 2-inch pieces, and shape them into little crescents. Bake on a well-greased cookie sheet at 350 degrees for 18 to 20 minutes.

Makes 12 to 15 cakes

MAIN MEAL TREATS

Morning Quiche

While most holiday recipe sections offer tons of ideas for dinner entrées and sweet-tooth blues, very little attention is paid to the fact that we still have to eat breakfast. That being the case, this quiche provides the perfect solution. It's healthy, hearty, and your family will love it.

- 4 eggs, well beaten
- 1½ cups heavy cream
- 1½ cups shredded cheddar cheese
- 1 teaspoon dried thyme
- 1 teaspoon dried oregano
- ½ teaspoon salt
- ½ teaspoon pepper
- ½ teaspoon garlic powder
- ¼ cup finely chopped onion
- ¼ cup chopped black olives
- ½ cup cooked, crumbled, and drained bacon or sausage (substitute cubed or shredded ham, if desired)
- 1 9-inch deep dish pie crust

Line pastry shell with aluminum foil. Bake at 400 degrees for 5 minutes. Remove foil. Bake at same temperature for additional 5 to 7 minutes, until nearly done. Remove from oven. Reduce oven temperature to 325 degrees. While pie crust is in oven, cook and drain bacon. Beat eggs, then add cream, seasoning, chopped onion, and olives. Mix in cheese. Crumble bacon and stir into the mixture; pour into the piecrust. Bake for 45 minutes to 1 hour. Quiche is done when toothpick inserted in the center of the quiche is dry when removed. Allow to set 10 to 15 minutes before slicing and serving.

Serves 6

Latkes (Potato Pancakes)
(Eastern European)

Potatoes have served as the basis in Eastern European Jewish cuisine for many years. Fried foods are traditionally savored around Hanukkah time (mid-December), since oil played a central role in the miracle Jews celebrate during the holiday. Latkes are one of the most typical dishes served by the Ashkenazim, as the Jews with roots in Eastern Europe are called. Many families hold their celebrations in front of the menorah, the nine-armed candelabra, while plates of latkes, sour cream, and apple sauce enjoy a central place on the dinner table nearby.

- 10 medium-large potatoes
- 2 onions
- 2 eggs
- ½ cup flour or matzah meal (available in the kosher sections of larger grocery stores)
- Salt and pepper, to taste
- Parsley or dill (optional)
- Vegetable oil (peanut or olive oil work best)

Peel potatoes and place them in a bowl filled with salt water until you are ready to grate them (this will keep them from turning brown). Grate the potatoes until they are almost the consistency of batter. If you desire, grate some of the potatoes coarsely and the remainder finely; this allows for a more complex consistency in the pancakes.

Grate the potatoes and onions separately; this is another way to keep the ingredients from turning brown. Combine when you have finished grating both. Squeeze out all the water you can into a separate bowl, but retain as much of the starch as possible in the mixture. Whip together potato/onion batter with eggs, flour, and spices.

Warm about ½ inch of oil in a frying pan. When a small piece of the batter can be set in the oil and turns brown all the way through, it is hot enough to fry the pancakes. Spoon about 1 tablespoon of batter into the pan at a time to make 1 pancake.

The latkes should be eaten hot, but they can be kept warm in the oven. They can also be frozen—just reheat in the oven or microwave. Latkes should be served with applesauce and sour cream.

Serves 12 as an appetizer or 6 as a main course

Spanish Turkey Soup

(Spanish)

This delectable soup recipe was contributed by Kitty Gamarra. In Spain, many families eat a midnight meal on Christmas Eve to celebrate the coming of the Christ-child. Traditionally, this soup serves as the main course.

- 2 cups turkey (raw or cooked, chopped if you prefer, with or without bones)
  Turkey liver, cooked (either baked with bird or lightly fried)
- 1 15-ounce can garbanzo beans (or 1 cup soaked raw garbanzos)
- 1 chopped onion
- 3 cloves of garlic
- 2 chicken bouillon cubes
- 1 tablespoons ham stock base (available in grocery stores)
- 10 cups of water
- 2 ounces (3 round bunches) angel hair noodles
- 1 thinly sliced, hard boiled egg
  Sprigs of fresh mint
- 1 lemon
  Salt and pepper, to taste

If using raw ingredients: Simmer raw turkey and raw garbanzos in 10 cups of water for 1 hour. Saute liver in olive oil until well browned, then mash with a fork to form a paste. Add the liver, onion, and bouillon to the turkey and broth.

If using cooked ingredients: Add cooked turkey, liver paste, onion, and bouillon to water. Add salt and pepper to taste, then allow to simmer for 30 minutes. Stir in the canned garbanzo beans and ham stock, then simmer for another 30 minutes. Stir in the egg slices and allow to simmer another 15 or 20 minutes. Add the angel hair noodles and cook for another 5 minutes.

This soup should be served hot. Squeeze juice from fresh lemon slices into individual servings. Add a sprig of fresh mint, too. It's traditional—and fun!—to drag the mint through the soup, allow it to soak slightly, and then remove it.

Serves 8 to 10

Ole' South Duck

Although turkey and ham still provide the traditional entrées for winter holiday dinners, it's often fun to serve something a little less conventional. (This is especially true if you have hunters in the family and wind up with a vast assortment of wild game in your freezer!) If that's the case, try this recipe. It's hearty enough to serve your family, and elegant enough to serve at the most formal of sit-down dinners.

2 ducks, skinned and quartered
¾ cup (1½ sticks) butter
2 large cans mushrooms
1 small bunch green onions, chopped
¼ cup fresh chopped thyme
2 cups water
3 tablespoons flour

In a large skillet, brown the ducks in ¼ cup of butter. Place the ducks on a rack in a roasting pan and set aside. Add the rest of the butter to the skillet. Stir in the mushrooms, onions, and thyme. Sauté over low heat until the onions become translucent (about 10 minutes). Pour the mixture over the ducks. Sprinkle with salt and pepper to taste. Pour 2 cups of water over ducks. Cover the pan and bake for approximately 2 hours at 300 degrees. When the duck is tender, remove it from the pan; reserve the vegetables and drippings.

Heat the mushroom and onion mixture on top of the stove; stir constantly with a wire whisk and gradually add the flour to make gravy. Cook the gravy over medium heat until it boils and thickens, continuing to stir constantly. Place the duck back in the pan and serve with wild rice.

Serves 8

Runja

(Polish)

Contributed by Kathy Pruchnicki, this Runja recipe was brought over from Poland by her husband's family in the late nineteenth century; this special dish was only prepared during the holiday season. Why? Because fresh meat was considered a luxury—a luxury so expensive that it could only be served at Christmastime.

- 2 loaves frozen bread dough (thaw and allow to rise according to package directions)
- 1½ pounds hamburger
- 1 large onion, diced
- 1 medium head cabbage
- Salt and pepper to taste

Brown hamburger and onion, then drain. Cut cabbage as you would for cole slaw but not as fine; boil until tender. Drain cabbage well and mix with the hamburger. Slice raised bread dough into even slices (about 7). Put a portion of mixture into each bread slice and fold over and crimp edges so it is sealed well. Put on greased cookie sheet and let rise for 1 hour. When risen, put into oven at 350 degrees and bake for 25 to 30 minutes—they should be golden brown. Brush tops with oil or melted butter.

Makes 7 servings

Quick Yeast Rolls

No holiday dinner would be complete without bread of one type or another. While you can always add rolls of the brown-and-serve variety, this season calls for something a little more special. That's where this recipe comes in. Total preparation time is 1 hour from start to finish, but don't tell anybody. These are so good that your family will think you've been slaving in the kitchen all day!

- 2 packages dry yeast
- ¼ cup warm water
- 3 tablespoons sugar, divided
- 1 egg, beaten
- 1¼ cups scalded milk, cooled
- 3 tablespoons melted butter
- ½ teaspoon salt
- 4 cups flour

Dissolve the yeast in the warm water and add 1 tablespoon of sugar. Set aside so the yeast can activate. In a large bowl, combine egg, milk, butter, the remaining 2 tablespoons sugar, and salt. Add yeast mixture and beat with a wire whisk until thoroughly blended. Add flour one cup at a time, then cover the bowl with a damp towel and place in a warm spot to rest for 15 minutes.

Turn dough out onto a floured pastry sheet and knead until smooth and elastic (about 5 minutes). Divide dough into 12 equal pieces and roll into balls. Place in large greased baking pan or cookie sheet, then cover loosely with a hot, damp towel. Place the pan in a warm spot until the rolls rise to double their size, usually about 30 minutes. Heat oven to 400 degrees. Bake until tops turn golden, about 20 minutes. Brush roll tops with melted butter and serve.

Makes 12 large rolls or 24 medium-sized rolls

Broccoli with Cheddar Sauce

This recipe became a Yuletide tradition in my household years ago. Why? For one thing, it's easy and elegant. But the main reason is much more simple. Even kids who don't like vegetables are so entranced by the cheddar sauce that they can't help but gobble it right up!

    1 large bag broccoli spears
    ½ cup (1 stick) butter
       Salt and pepper to taste
    4 tablespoons flour (approximate)
    1 cup milk (approximate)
    2 cups shredded cheddar cheese

Prepare the broccoli according to package directions. Melt the butter over medium heat and sprinkle in a little salt and pepper. Stir constantly with a fork; add enough flour to make a paste the consistency of cake frosting. Continue to stir as you add the milk. Boil and stir for 1 minute. (If the sauce is thicker than cream gravy, you may need to add a little more milk.) Remove from heat and stir in the cheese until it melts. Pour over well-drained broccoli and serve immediately.

Serves 6 to 8

FESTIVE BEVERAGES

CROCKPOT WASSAIL

(English)

A terrific variation of the ancient wassail mixture (for more information, see chapter 2), this hot concoction just begs to be consumed. You won't want to forget about your friends, the apple trees, though. Just set some wassail aside to cool, blend in an egg, then run outside to get the tree asperging ritual underway.

8 cups apple juice or cider
2 cups cranberry juice
¾ cup sugar
1 teaspoon allspice
2 cinnamon sticks
1 orange
Whole cloves

Turn the crockpot on high and pour in the apple and cranberry juices. Stir in the sugar and allspice, then add cinnamon sticks. Stud the orange with the cloves—about 25 to 30 cloves should do the trick—and toss it in. Cover the pot and cook on high for 1 hour. Change the setting to low and allow to simmer for 3 more hours, then serve.

Serves 10

Coffee with Kahlúa & Cream

Since I'm a coffee-holic, no holiday celebration would be complete for me without a great cup of java. Even if you're not the coffee connoisseur that I am, though, give this beverage a whirl. It provides the perfect end to any holiday meal.

- 4 cups hot brewed coffee
- ¼ cup Irish Cream liqueur
- ¼ cup Kahlúa
- Sugar (optional)
- Whipped cream

Pour hot coffee, Kahlúa, and Irish Cream into a heatproof pitcher and mix well. Pour mixture into mugs and add sugar if desired. Garnish with whipped cream.

Note: For a nonalcoholic version, buy flavored syrups, but use a smaller amount of syrup than liqueur.

Serves 4

 Sherbet Frappé

(French)

Frappé—an old French holiday favorite—was originally a slushy, partially frozen fruit juice drink. Someone improved upon that recipe many years ago, however, and came up with the terrific punch offering found below. Because it's so creamy and scrumptious, my family has enjoyed it during the holidays for generations. Once your family gets a taste, I guarantee that they will love it, too.

- Large bottles of chilled ginger ale (the amount necessary depends upon the size of your punch bowl)
- 1 half gallon carton of lime or orange sherbet
- Punchbowl

A few minutes before serving time, fill the punchbowl about ¾ full with cold ginger ale. With an ice cream tool, scoop the sherbet into balls. Add them to the bowl, allowing them to float on top of the ginger ale. Ladle into cups and serve.

Serving size depends upon the initial amount of ginger ale used

Hot Buttered Rum

After a hectic day of fighting holiday traffic on the streets and in the stores, we all need a little time to relax and unwind—and nothing seems to do the trick better than a steaming mug of hot buttered rum. Because it's also delicious without the alcohol, it serves as the perfect "before bed" drink for little folks.

1 quart apple juice
¼ cup (½ stick) butter
¼ cup dark corn syrup
　Nutmeg
1 ounce dark rum (optional)
　Cinnamon sticks

Pour juice into a glass or metal pot. Add butter and syrup. Stir constantly while you heat on stove until butter melts and the mixture is steaming hot. Do not allow to boil! Pour into large mugs, sprinkle with nutmeg, and add rum if desired. Serve with a cinnamon stick.

Serves 6

Culinary Miscellany

Holiday Orange Treat

Symbolically, this is the ultimate in Winter Solstice treats. The peppermint stick reminds us that winter must come before the Sun (which is represented by the orange) can take form in the sky and warm us with His radiance.

- 1 chilled orange
- 1 peppermint stick

Wash the orange thoroughly, then with a sharp knife, carefully cut a small "x" into the rind. Insert the peppermint stick into the "x." Use it as a straw and drink the orange juice through it.

Serves 1

Quick Party Sandwich Spread

If your children are anything like mine, they tend to forget things until the very last minute—especially when it comes to important things like needing a loaf of sandwiches for the school party. Now there's help! This spread takes less than five minutes to prepare, and the results are spectacular.

- ¾ cup salad olives, drained and finely minced
- ½ cup finely chopped pecans or walnuts
- 16 ounces softened cream cheese
- 2–3 tablespoons mayonnaise
  Green food coloring (optional)

Place all ingredients in a food processor and mix until smooth. Stir in a few drops of green food coloring for a festive look.

Makes 1 loaf of sandwiches

Stuffed Celery

Because Yule is a busy time of year, I always keep a batch of stuffed celery in the fridge. It not only provides the perfect hors d'oeuvre for unexpected company, but makes a great snack for kids when mealtimes don't run on schedule.

- 1 bunch of celery
- 4 tablespoons mayonnaise
- 8 ounces softened cream cheese
- Paprika

Wash the celery and cut the stalks into pieces about 2 to 3 inches long. Mix the mayonnaise and cream cheese together, then spread on celery. Sprinkle liberally with paprika.

Serves 8 to 10

Snow Cream

If you're fortunate enough to live in an area where snow is prevalent during the season, give this recipe a shot. It's not only easy enough for kids to make, but will give them a reason to come inside and warm up after a full day of playing outdoors.

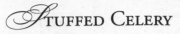

- 1 bowl of snow (use clean fresh snow from outdoors!)
- ¼ teaspoon vanilla extract
- ¼–½ cup sugar
- Heavy cream

Stir the sugar and vanilla extract into the snow. Add cream a little at a time until the mixture is slushy, then serve.

Serves 1

REINDEER SANDWICHES

These little sandwiches look just like Rudolph the Red-Nosed Reindeer. They're not only a snap to fix, but are guaranteed to put everybody in the holiday spirit.

1 slice bread for each sandwich
Peanut butter
Pretzels
Raisins
Marshmallows or maraschino cherries

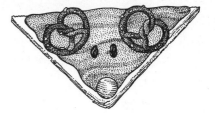

Spread the bread liberally with peanut butter, then with a sharp knife, cut it diagonally in half to make 2 pieces. Place 1 large pretzel in each corner of the diagonal cut to form antlers, 2 raisins in the center of the triangle for eyes, and 1 marshmallow or cherry below the eyes for the nose.

Serves 1

COFFEE SPOONS

Nothing adds a touch of festivity to coffee and hot chocolate any better than candied coffee spoons. They're so tasty and elegant that you may even want to give them as gifts!

Plastic spoons
Milk chocolate morsels
Powdered sugar
Chocolate sprinkles
Granulated sugar
Waxed paper

Melt the morsels in the microwave (place them in a microwave-safe dish and microwave on high 20 to 30 seconds, stirring until melted). Dip the spoon bowls in the chocolate mixture, allowing the chocolate to travel part way up the spoon stem. Dip some of the coated spoons in powdered sugar, some in chocolate sprinkles, and some in granulated sugar. Allow to set on waxed paper, then use to stir coffee or hot chocolate.

Note: If you'd like to give these as gifts, wrap individual spoons (when cool) in colored cellophane and tie with bits of ribbon.

PART IV

CREATING PERSONAL TRADITIONS

THE DAWNING OF SOLSTICE

T'was the dawning of Solstice
The shortest day of the year
And we cheered on the Mother
For Her delivery was near
And as we watched the pink streaks
That flashed bright in the sky
We knew He was coming
In the flash of an eye
Then the Mother groaned once
And an orange streak appeared
Then yellow, then white
And we all laughed and cheered
Then the first ray of sunshine
Bathed us all with its light
And we knew that the Sun
Had been born of the Night
And He rose in the sky—Just a tiny bright ball—
To warm our hearts and our planet . . .
Happy Solstice to all!

—ADAPTED BY DOROTHY MORRISON FROM THE 1823 POEM
"A VISIT FROM ST. NICHOLAS" BY CLEMENT C. MOORE

17

PERSONAL TRADITIONS

GROWING UP IN A CHRISTIAN home, Christmas was a big deal for me. Like every child, I daydreamed of Santa and envisioned all the goodies he might bring. It was a fun time. A wondrous time. The kind of time that magic is made of. What made the season so special for me, though, really had little to do with Santa. It was the personal traditions that my parents used to gift wrap the season—the customs that seemed to belong to my family alone.

For us, the winter holidays began on Thanksgiving Day just after dinner, and lasted through January 1. We'd start by putting up the Christmas tree. Daddy strung the lights—it had to be done just so—while we unpacked the ornaments and decorations. The all-afternoon affair involved popcorn-stringing, cookie-baking, tree-decorating, and animated discussions of Christmases past. (Of course, this always included the story of how Mama nearly burned down the house the year she decided to put real candles on the tree!) It was a fun-filled, magical day that didn't end until every corner of our home was transformed into a spectacular holiday vision.

On December 2, we'd make a list of all the good and bad things we'd done over the year, add it to our Christmas list, and leave it on the kitchen table for St. Nicholas. Why? Because we had to show St. Nick that we were trustworthy. He came for his main visit on December 6 (St. Nicholas Day), and he only left switches and ashes for dishonest children. When the day finally dawned we'd hang our stockings in the kitchen and leave for school. That evening, in the midst of supper, we'd hear a loud crash in the living room and know that St. Nick had arrived. Our hardwood floor would be covered with the apples, oranges, nuts, and hard candy that he'd thrown through the window because we'd been so good. We'd gather the goodies in paper bags (he usually supplied those, too) then head back to the kitchen to check our stockings. Sure enough, they were crammed full—and with enough tiny gifts and novelties to make any child glow.

The next eighteen days were full, too. We sent cards. We shopped. We baked. We made last-minute gifts and created new decorations for the following year. Somehow in the midst of all the hubbub, we still managed to find time for holiday parties and group caroling expeditions to the nursing homes and hospitals.

Finally, Christmas Eve rolled around. After eating a grand supper of fried oysters and boiled shrimp, my sisters and I would head upstairs to await Santa's appearance. We'd wait for what seemed an eternity; then finally, we'd hear the signal—the tinkle of bells that meant Santa had arrived. Every year we rushed downstairs in hopes of getting a tiny glimpse of him, but instead, we'd find only our parents and a room full of presents.

After we settled down a bit, Daddy read the story of the Christ-child from the bible. Mama followed with "The Night Before Christmas," and then the fun began. We opened the presents, laughed and played, drank eggnog and cider from crystal cups, and as things wound down, sang our favorite carols. We attended the midnight church service and ate a big breakfast afterward. Then before falling into bed, we hung up our stockings. (Somehow, Santa always managed to visit our house twice before daybreak!)

Christmas Day brought a traditional turkey dinner that was served on Mama's best china. There was a toast as we uncorked the pear wine Daddy and I had made the summer before. For dessert, there was mincemeat pie, pecan divinity, assorted cookies, and whiskey pralines. It was a delightful celebration of abundance. Of course, we all ate too much and the afternoon was spent in an effort to recuperate.

I've since grown up, gotten married, and moved away. While we still practice many of those traditions, my husband and I have formed a few of our own. The winter holidays still begin for us on Thanksgiving Day and St. Nick still pays his annual visit. Since I'm Pagan and he's Christian, though, we now celebrate both the Winter Solstice and Christmas.

We kick off Solstice with a morning apple juice toast to the Old Year, saying something like:

> *Winter day of longest night*
> *Step aside now for the light*
> *Thank you for the things you've brought*
> *That only darkness could have wrought*

Then we name off the gifts of darkness—regeneration, peace, dreams, organization, quietude, and so on—and drink the juice.

That evening, we set the Yule log ablaze; we start it from a bit of last year's log, settle in front of the fire, sip hot buttered rum, and toast the Sun by saying something like:

> *Old King, we thank You for all You've done*
> *For lessons learned, and victories won*
> *We must, however, bid You adieu*
> *For Your reign is finished—'tis over and through*
> *Come forth, Young King of newest light*
> *Be born with ease; grow strong and bright*
> *Gain strength and stature in the sky*
> *Shed Your warmth on us now from on high*

Afterward, we make silent wishes for the coming year and exchange gifts; the next morning, we toast the Sun with orange juice saying something like:

O Newborn Sun of love and light
Rise quickly now, rise high and bright
Gain power in the sky above
We grant you our support and love

The orange juice toasts continue daily until Christmas Eve. So does the gift exchange, with each person getting one present a day. The gift-giving reaches its grand finale on Christmas Eve, when Santa sneaks in and fills our home with packages. We always remember to hang our stockings, for even after all these years, Santa still manages to visit my home twice!

Christmas Day is spent with close friends of ours. Neither my family nor theirs has relatives in the area, so we adopted each other when we moved to Missouri. We take turns fixing Christmas dinner, and spend the rest of the day wrapped in the warmth and joy of friendship.

Our holidays don't end with Christmas Day, though. New Year's Day is a big deal, too. Along with the traditional pot of black-eyed peas, I fix an herbed, buttered, and gravied delicacy I call Ole' South Duck (included in the recipe section). I

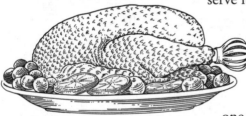

serve it with wild rice, homemade bread, assorted veggies, and desserts to the families of all my husband's duck-hunting buddies. Much to my surprise, this fairly new tradition—a dinner that began with five people and has somehow grown into over thirty attendees—has become one of the major social events of the year. While I'd like to think that my culinary skills are responsible, I know better. It's the special camaraderie, the friendship, and the idea of sharing and marking a brand new year together that keeps them coming back for more.

Our holiday traditions work well for us, but they probably wouldn't hold the same special meaning or significance for anyone else. For this reason, people all over the world create their own. Take my friend Anne Marie, for example. Her Minnesota celebration revolves around the Solstice itself, and begins the night before. After the lighting of the Yule log, there's an all-night vigil to ensure that the fire is fueled properly and doesn't go out.

Her family wakes promptly at 6:00 A.M. on Solstice morning, then drives to the University of Minnesota footbridge that hovers over the Mississippi River. There they join the throng of folks who await the Sun's birth and the first streaks of blazing pink and orange that rip through the cold, dark winter sky. They sing songs to the night, the Great Mother, the newborn baby Sun, and the returning light. They hold hands and perform circle dances, hop up and down, and verbally urge the Mother to birth Her Sun. And then, amidst cheers and screams and shouts of "Push! Push!" the light spills forth and reflects its jubilant brilliance upon the river. The Sun is born and light is returned to the world.

Its joyful midwives—exhilarated, exhausted, and ravenous all at the same time—continue the celebration at a nearby coffee shop, where they exchange gifts and eat breakfast. After all, birthing a baby the size of the Sun is hard work. Anyone capable of such a feat is definitely deserving of a hearty meal, a terrific gift and, if they don't have to rush off to work, an extra eight hours of sleep!

No matter how you celebrate the holidays, personal traditions are important. They make families feel special and bring a magic to the season that's theirs alone. Best of all, they aren't hard to create. It's simply a matter of thinking creatively and then following through. Take our New Year's dinner, for instance—it was a spur of the moment idea that grew into something we'd never imagined. Not only has it become one of our traditions, but a much looked-forward-to custom for all the families involved. Your personal family traditions can easily gain the same stature, just don't be afraid to try something new or vary from the expected path.

18

DAILY EVENT CALENDAR

A CALENDAR OF DAILY CELEBRATION ideas for the holiday season is included in this chapter. Every effort has been made to place specific festivals on their appropriate dates. However, the dates on this calendar are not carved in stone. Why? Because certain festival dates and the Full Moon vary from year to year, and historians can't seem to agree on others. For that reason, you may find that I've listed certain celebrations on days that aren't in sync with your personal festival dates. Should that occur, please feel free to celebrate the daily holidays whenever they seem most appropriate to you.

That having been said, use the calendar to grab some holiday spirit, honor the Deities, and welcome the returning light. Rejoice, laugh, and have fun. After all, that's the stuff that personal tradition is born of!

DECEMBER 1

Today belongs to Poseidon, the Greek god of oceans and seas. Begin the day with a family toast of water to Poseidon by saying something like:

Great God of the ocean and seas and rebirth
We honor You now for Your value and worth
As we take this fresh day and we start life anew
Watch over and bless us in all that we do

Since Poseidon is also the god of rebirth, this day also provides a great time to tie up loose ends, complete projects, and take appropriate steps to turn over a new leaf. Make it a family project, then treat yourselves by incorporating something different into your lives: Go somewhere you've never been, try a new dish, or play a new game. What you do really doesn't matter. What's important is that you try something different as a measure of rebirth and that you make it fun. Who knows? You just may start a personal tradition that belongs to your family alone!

This is also a good day to make your holiday card lists. Make it a family event. Start with a discussion about how greeting cards let others know we're thinking of them and how they bring smiles and good cheer. Add the names of those you think may be especially lonely during the winter holidays.

DECEMBER 2

The Japanese celebrate Hari No Kuyo (the Festival of Broken Needles) today. It's a day to reclaim the feminine arts and enjoy them. Follow suit by working on small arts and crafts or needlework projects. This also makes it a good day to work on holiday gifts or decorations. (For ideas, see the appropriate sections of this book.)

This is also the day that St. Nicholas sneaks into homes to determine whether the children who live there are honest. If you have children, help them to make small lists of their accomplishments over the last year—especially if you plan to celebrate St. Nick's Day.

Take some time today, too, to sign, address, and stamp your holiday cards. When the cards are ready for the mail, stack them up and enchant them by saying something like:

Good luck and wishes we bestow
Within these cards before they go
With love and joy we set this spell
And send it through the mail to gel

DECEMBER 3

Today is the Roman festival of Bona Dea, the patroness of women. Traditionally only celebrated by women, this is a terrific day to have a short get-together with the female sector of your family. Serve hot apple cider and sit around the table. Remember your foremothers and discuss the traits they've passed on to you. Talk about other women who have influenced your life. Then hold hands and take turns expressing your thoughts on womanhood and what it means to you. Finish by toasting Bona Dea. Say something like:

Great Goddess of Women, Creatrix above
We send You our thanks—and our laughter and love—
For this gift You've bestowed upon all in this room
A common thread in Life's Tapestry weaved on Your loom

Today also marks the Greek festival of Rhea, Great Mother of the Earth. Since grains are generally used in this celebration, it provides an excellent opportunity to do some family baking. Pies, cakes, cookies, and bread are all good choices. Before you mix the ingredients, take some time to thank Rhea by saying something like:

Rhea, Great Mother of Earth and Her bounty
We offer our thanks for Your grains, fruits, and seeds
We thank you for sharing your wondrous abundance
And for tending our bodies' nutritional needs

DECEMBER 4

Today belongs to Pallas Athena, the Goddess of Arts and Wisdom. It's a good day to finish your shopping or make holiday gifts and decorations. Before you begin, though, light a yellow candle and say the following prayer to Pallas Athena. It's guaranteed to wrap you in Her blessings all day!

Gracious Goddess of Wisdom and Art
Rain Your blessings upon this new day we start
Grant Your guidance and wisdom in all that we do
For today is your day, and we give it to You

December 5

Because today marks the Festival of Chango (the Santerian/Yoruban God of the Human Spirit), it provides an excellent time to embrace positive changes and build confidence in others. Let go of negativity, resolve differences, and do something nice for someone else. Make positive changes in your life, too. Ask Chango for help in these matters by chanting something like:

Chango, God of Humankind
Help me see where I was blind
Fill my heart with joy and light
My mind with resolution bright
Let human spirit thrive and grow
And become a beacon all shall know
So even in the darkest night
We shed Your rays of guiding light

December 6

This is the day that St. Nicholas visits the world's children and leaves them treats. If you don't want to go to all the trouble that my folks did, just let your children hang their stockings in the morning, then fill them with fruit, nuts, and small gifts before they return from school.

Because this day is also sacred to Odin, another idea might be to have a family "rune exploration" night. Hide runes about the house, then allow family members to search for them. When all the stones have been found, give each person a short reading from the runes they've gathered. For those of you unfamiliar with rune meanings, a short list of definitions follows. (For definitions of a more comprehensive nature, check for books in your local library.)

Feoh: Success, gain
Ur: Growth, transformation
Thorn: Defense, passage
Ansur: Communication
Rad: Travel, spontaneity
Ken: Creativity
Geofu: Union, partnership
Wynn: Wishes granted
Hagall: Chaos, change
Nied: Endurance, stability
Is: Standstill
Jara: Rewards, gifts

Yr: Discovery
Peorth: Awareness
Eolh: Protection, bravery
Sigel: Victory
Tir: Commitment
Beorc: Birth of ideas
Eoh: Change, flexibility
Mann: Relationships
Lagu: Intuition, magic
Ing: Preparation
Daeg: Emergence, growth
Othel: Ancestry

DECEMBER 7

On this day, the Turks honor the Melvana, fairy-like spirits who some folks liken to the whirling dervishes of the cosmos. If the holiday preparations are getting you down, or there just aren't enough hours in the day, take a handful of dried thyme and go outside. Hold the herbs tightly in your hand and ask the Melvana to help you by chanting something like:

> *Twirling spirits—whirling sprites*
> *Aid me, now, and make work light*
> *You are many—I am one*
> *Do your stuff; let's get things done*

Blow the thyme from your hand, watch it fall to the ground, then get to work. You'll be finished before you know it!

DECEMBER 8

On this day, the Egyptians celebrate the festival of Neith, the Goddess from whom the sun first rose. The Japanese also celebrate the birth of the Sun goddess, Amaterasu, today. Give Them Their due by rising early this morning and chanting something like:

Great Goddess, Neith, Who birthed the Sun
That shines on us 'til day is done
And Amaterasu, Golden Globe
Who wraps us warmly in Her robe
We give our thanks to You this day
Please bless us in our work and play

If you feel you've been mistreated in some way, this is also a good day for rectification. Why? Because today is also sacred to Astraea, the Greek Goddess of Justice. Ask Her to set things straight by lighting a purple candle and chanting something like:

Astraea! Impartial, objective One!
Right the wrong that has been done
Bring me justice—bring it now
In whatever manner You'll allow
Queen of Justice, hear my plea
As I will, so mote it be

DECEMBER 9

Today marks the first day of Daikon Daki, a Japanese festival in which radishes are cooked for those visiting Kyoto's Royotokuji Temple. Symbolically, this is a celebration of darkness and light, for radishes (light-colored orbs) are born from the dark fertile womb of the Earth. Celebrate by serving radishes at mealtime. Enchant them by saying something like:

Little orbs so like the Sun
Birthed from Darkness, every one
Fill our hearts with warmth and light
And bring us joy with every bite

The Mexican goddess Tonatzin, the Mother of Health, is also honored with a festival today. Celebrate by serving apples for dessert and asking Her continual blessings on your family. Before you bite in, say something like:

Oh great Tonatzin, Mother of Health
Thank you for nurturing us with Your wealth
Bless our health and keep us well
As we eat these apples and seal the spell

DECEMBER 10

On this day, the French turn out to honor Liberty, the Goddess of Freedom. The Romans honor Her, too, in a festival known as Lux Mundi, which means "light of the world." Join them in celebration by having a discussion about freedom and what it means to each family member. Then ask your family to take steps toward getting rid of negative associations or situations that restrict their personal progress. (If you have children on restriction, start the ball rolling by ungrounding them!) Afterward, light a white candle in honor of Liberty. As it burns, chant something like:

Gracious Goddess, Liberty
Guide our paths, and help us see
Grant our wishes, dreams, and hopes
Cast aside our personal ropes
Bring us strength and make us free
This we ask You, Liberty

This is also the day that Eskimos pay homage to the spirits of slaughtered whales. For that reason, don't eat fish today, and give thanks to all the water creatures who have fed you in the last year. Toast them with a glass of water, saying something like:

By scale and gill and tail and fin
We give you thanks, all watery friends
For giving of yourselves that we
Might eat and never hungry be
We honor you and send our love
With fondest wishes from Earth above

DECEMBER 11

Today marks the Roman festival of Bruma, the Goddess of Winter. If you live in a snowy area, go outside and make a snow goddess. Lie on the ground and make snow angels. Go sledding. Have snowball fights. Enjoy the beauty of the day and thank Bruma for the winter wonder She's created for you. Wrap up the fun by bringing some snow indoors and making snow cream. (See Chapter 16 for the recipe.)

If Bruma doesn't bless your area with snow, serve your family Bruma ice cream figures today. Just place two scoops of vanilla ice cream (one on top of the other) in a cone or dish, and use red hot candies for her facial features. For hair, use candy sprinkles or bits of red licorice rope. Before eating, thank Bruma by saying something like:

Winter Goddess, Winter Queen
We give You thanks for icy sheen
For the beauty in which You wrap the Earth
As dreams invade Her spacious girth
For tending this season peacefully
We honor You, Bruma! Blessed be

DECEMBER 12

Mexicans celebrate the Feast of Our Lady of Guadalupe (Tonatzin, the Black Madonna) today. Apparently, the Lady appeared to Juan Diego on a Mexican mountaintop on this date in 1531 and asked him to rebuild the temple that had once stood there. Thinking She was the Virgin Mary, he went to the Christian clergy with Her request. The clergy didn't believe him, so the Lady let them know She meant business by causing flowers to bloom out of season in the spot. She is the patroness of Mexico, the Americas, and children, especially those unborn.

Take some time today to ask the Lady to bless the members of your family and to encourage the birth of the Sun. Light a blue candle in Her honor and say something like:

Blessed Madonna, Mother of All
Hear us now and heed our call
Watch over us from up above
And bless us with your constant love
Urge the Sun's birth in the sky
So He shines brightly from on high
Blessed Mother, hear our plea
As we will, so mote it be

DECEMBER 13

December 13 is a big day with lots of things to celebrate. For one thing, it's the Feast of St. Lucia (the Christianized version of the Sun Goddess, Lucina), known in some areas as "the light of the world." In Sweden, the oldest daughter of each family represents the melting winter and growing days by dressing in white, wearing a wreath of candles on her head, and serving her parents a breakfast of saffroned rolls and coffee. While a headdress of candles certainly stirs the romantic in all of us, clearly, it isn't safe. Instead, dress in light colors and have a candlelit breakfast to celebrate. Serve biscuits (add some yellow food coloring if you like), eggs sunny-side up, and orange juice. Encourage the Sun to grow by saying something like:

Coldest Darkness, melt away
Sunlight, grow, and with us stay
Warm our bodies, hearts, and Earth
And guide our paths in joy and mirth

Koto-Hajime, the Japanese festival of beginnings, also occurs today. It not only provides an excellent time to turn over a new leaf and start something new, but to make peace and put old things to rest. I like to celebrate by working magic to break bad habits. If this appeals to you, the following spell will jump-start your willpower. Just write down the habit and burn the paper in a fireproof dish while chanting:

(Habit), be gone as paper burns
Urges, be quiet—you cannot churn
I cannot hear you anymore
You are gone—I've barred the door

Flush the ashes down the toilet or throw them in a running body of water.

Today marks the beginning of the Runic half-month of Jara as well, which symbolizes the completion of the cosmic cycle and the joining of forces between the mundane and spiritual worlds. This makes it a great day for wish magic. Just write your wish—or draw a symbol of it—on the back of a bay leaf. Then strike a match, light the leaf, and leave it to burn in a fireproof dish. Your wish will soar into the cosmos and take immediate steps toward manifestation.

Finally, the Greeks pay homage to Demeter today as She tends seeds and roots in the dark womb of the Earth. To celebrate, serve a supper of vegetables and grains tonight. Before you eat, honor Demeter by saying something like:

> *Great Goddess of all plants on Earth*
> *Who tends the crops that fill its girth*
> *We ask your blessing on this meal*
> *And honor You in turning Wheel*

DECEMBER 14

This is the first day of Halcyon Days, a Greek festival to honor the Kingfisher Goddess, Alcyone. This celebration lasts for fourteen days and marks the time when the seas become calm and peaceful. It is a time of peace for humankind as well. Celebrate by refusing to argue and bicker. Start each day by asking for Alcyone's blessing. Say something like:

> *Smiles and joy, goodwill and peace*
> *Alcyone, I ask You, please*
> *Let these shine from within me*
> *And touch all those I meet and see*

Make a game of it by charging each family member a nickel, dime, or quarter each time they say a cross word. At the end of Halcyon Days, donate the money to a favorite charity.

Today also marks Soyal, a Hopi festival honoring Spider Woman, the Goddess of Creation. This makes it a great day to use your imagination, begin projects, and put ideas into action. I like to honor Spider Woman by working on magical holiday gifts like bath salts, candles, and so forth. If this appeals to you, gather your materials and ask Spider Woman's blessing before you begin, saying something like:

Spider Woman, Creative One
You Who birthed the Moon and Sun
Inspire and bless me as I work
Smooth out each problem and each quirk
So that creative juices flow
As I will, it shall be so

December 15

The Full Moon closest to Winter Solstice is known as the Oak Moon. The oak tree has long symbolized the male aspect of Divinity and the natural flow between the material and spiritual worlds. Its trunk and branches grow and stretch fervently toward the sky in the physical world, while its roots dig deeply into the hidden planes of the underworld. Even in the dormancy of winter, the oak hosts the new life of mistletoe sprouting from its branches—a reminder that life is always new, always fresh, and always constant.

As you celebrate the fullness of the Oak Moon, remember that you play just as an integral a part in the workings of the cosmos (the world that is not seen with the physical eye) as you do in the world you wake to everyday. Celebrate the return of the Divine Child and New Light by adorning your family with sprigs of mistletoe and giving each member a candle to remind them that they are each individual flames of the Coming Sun with their own paths to light.

December 16

Today marks the Roman and Greek festivals of the Goddesses of Wisdom, Sapientia and Sophia. Celebrate by playing mind-challenging, thinking games like Trivial Pursuit, Scrabble, or charades. If you have problems coming up with game answers, try this silent invocation:

Give me the answer, Wise Goddesses, two
And I'll honor You both when this game is through

If the goddesses help you, remember to light a candle in Their Honor.

If games aren't your thing, this is also a good day to think about positive solutions to any problems you may have. Ask Sapientia and Sophia to aid you; say something like:

> *Sapientia! Sophia! Goddesses Wise*
> *Bring quick resolution to this demise*
> *Grant me Your wisdom, Your savvy, and grace*
> *Bring positive answers so I can replace*
> *This negative energy that falls over me*
> *As I will, Wisest Ladies, so mote it be*

DECEMBER 17

Since today marks the first day of Saturnalia, it's a great time for a social. Invite people over for a potluck dinner, a gift exchange, or throw a costume party. Include the Lord of Misrule by allowing children to plan meal menus today. Better yet, make the Lord of Misrule a central figure in the celebration by choosing someone to dress in the role. Designate a special mug as the Cup of Change, and fill it with hot cider. Then give it to the Lord and have him approach attendees by asking them to embrace the changes in the Earth, the Sky, and themselves by drinking from it. Don't forget to honor Saturn, the God of Agriculture, Lessons, and Karmic Law. Have everyone choose a lesson they've learned over the past year—something that was especially tough to get through—and discuss it with the rest of the group. Not only will you save someone else the aggravation you went through, but you will lighten your own Karmic load dramatically. Start the discussion by chanting the following together:

> *Saturn, God of Lessons Learned*
> *And those to come—those yet unturned*
> *Help us lighten Karmic load*
> *By sharing what we've reaped and sowed*

DECEMBER 18

This is the day that the Latvians celebrate Winter Solstice. According to legend, four gift-bearing spirits appear at this time to herald the birth of Diev, the Sun God. The spirits are the Latvian version of Santa, and homes are decorated to welcome them and their charge. Celebrate by preparing a gift grabbag with one token for each person. Then honor Diev and his entourage by planting five daffodil or other yellow flowering bulbs in a shallow pot. Light a candle by the pot and bless the bulbs by saying something like:

> *Diev, I plant these bulbs for You*
> *As they sprout, You shall grow, too*
> *And when their blooms reach toward the sky*
> *Smile upon them from on high*

DECEMBER 19

Today is the Festival of Opalia, celebrated to honor Ops, the Roman Goddess of Grain and Agriculture. Since the growth of wheat is attributed to Her, this is an excellent day to work on your holiday baking. Another idea might be to have a bread breaking ritual. Bless the bread by chanting something like:

> *Good Goddess Ops, of wheat and grain*
> *We thank You for the knowledge gained*
> *To grow the wheat that made this bread*
> *The golden grain that keeps us fed*

Then ask each person to tear their slice in half. Each person must eat one-half while saying:

> *As bread is made from golden grain*
> *The Sun shall grow in strength again*

The other half should then be torn to shreds and placed on a central platter to be scattered outside for birds and other small animals. During the scattering, say something like:

We give you back unto the Earth
With joy and laughter, love and mirth
We do this now in Op's great name
To honor Her—hear our refrain!

Today also marks Pongol, the Hindu solstice celebration in honor of the Sun Goddess, Sankrat.

December 20

This is an excellent day for women to sit back and relax. Why? Because Tsao Chun, the Chinese Festival of the Kitchen God, is celebrated today, and it's customary for women to stay out of the kitchen. Comply—just for today—and let the men in your life take over the culinary and cleaning duties. Before they begin, ask them to ask the God's blessing by saying something like:

Kitchen God, now hear our plea
Help us whip up a delicacy
Let no dish be ruined or burn
Help us shine, for it's our turn

Today also marks the Norse festival of Mother Night—sometimes called Modres-Nach or Mudda Nacht—the Bringer of Prophetic Dreams. If you wish to see your future, start early in the evening by lighting a bayberry candle and placing a small piece of citrine and a sprig of mugwort under your pillow. Just before you go to sleep, put a notepad and pencil by the bed (you'll need these to write down your dreams later) and ask Mother Night to aid you by chanting:

Darkest Mother, Nighttime One
Aid me now that day is done
Bring me dreams that I might see
What You have in store for me

December 21

The Druidic celebration of Alban Arthuan occurs today. It's a festival in which gifts and charity are showered upon the poor. Do your part by making a contribution to your favorite charity, or by taking a gift or two down to the local homeless shelter.

Today is also the shortest day of the year, and marks Winter Solstice or Yule. Rise at dawn and dress in fire colors (yellow, gold, orange, or red), then ring bells to chase away the darkness. Hang sunflower heads on bare tree limbs to encourage the Sun and His feathered friends, and tie them with blue ribbons to honor His Mother, the Sky. When the dark of night falls, honor it with a farewell toast by saying something like:

Farewell, Darkness, you've served us well
You've brought peace and calmness with your spell
You've helped us regroup and regenerate, too
And for those reasons we honor you
The time has come, though, to say goodbye
Farewell, Darkness! Go now! Fly!

Then light the Yule log with a piece of last year's log, while chanting:

Goodbye Old King—hello, New
With this log we honor You
The old reign's gone—the new has begun
We welcome now the newborn Sun

When the flames begin to dance, write wishes on paper and toss them in the fire. Don't forget to kiss under the mistletoe, exchange gifts, and make merry. Above all, remember to save some Yule log ashes to boost your magic in the coming year!

Yule Rituals

Of course, no Yule book would be complete without some formalized Yule rituals. While I encourage spur-of-moment, spontaneous worship celebrations, that may not be your style. For this reason, I've included the rituals on the following pages.

If you decide to use these rites, I urge you to use them for guideline purposes only. Have fun. Be creative. Personalize them and make them your own. Remember: The more of yourself you put into magic, the more more you'll get out of it!

Ritual

    Small sprig of holly
1   oak leaf
1   bell (eastern quarter)
1   red candle (southern quarter)
    Small bowl of ice water (western quarter)
    A few acorns (northern quarter)
    Your choice of incense (optional)
    Yule log
    Your choice of cakes and drink

Gather wherever you plan to light the Yule log. Place the log in the center of the Circle area, and the bell, candle, water, and acorns in their respective quarters. If you opted for incense, light it as well. Then using the sprig of holly, cast the Circle in your usual manner. Go to the east, and invoke its quarter guardians by saying something like:

> *Spirits of the east, I conjure You*
> *Come into this Circle and stay 'til we're through*
> *Whirl and twirl 'til the magic has ceased*
> *We invite You. Come forth. Share our fun. Blessed be!*

Then walking clockwise around the Circle, ring the bell until you return to the eastern quarter.

Light the candle in the south and invoke its guardians by saying something like:

> *I conjure You now, O Spirits of Fire*
> *Spirits of Sun, of love and desire*
> *Illuminate our magic until it has ceased*
> *We invite You. Come forth. Share our fun. Blessed be!*

With the candle in hand, travel the Circle in a clockwise motion until you return to the southern quarter.

Invoke the guardians of the west by saying something like:

> *O Watery Spirits of the cold Winter chill*
> *Of ice and of sleet and of snow on the hills*
> *Flow with us now 'til the magic has ceased*
> *We invite You. Come forth. Share our fun. Blessed be!*

Walking clockwise, sprinkle the Circle with water.

Finally, call on the guardians of the north by saying something like:

> *O Spirits of Earth, I arouse You from sleep*
> *For You hold our roots in Your womb, warm and deep*
> *Bring our Circle Your richness 'til the magic has ceased*
> *We invite You. Come forth. Share our fun. Blessed be!*

Walk the Circle clockwise, sprinkling the acorns as you go.

Light the Yule log and wish upon its flame. As it burns, tell the tale of the Holly and Oak Kings, recounting their battle to the participants. Then honor both Kings by using the chants described in the Personal Traditions section, and tossing the holly sprig in the Yule fire. Afterward, pass the tray of cakes and ritual cup around the Circle while saying to each other:

> *On shortest day and longest night*
> *I give to you the warmth of light*

Close the ritual by dismissing the guardians. Begin in the east, and say something like:

> *We thank You for coming and attending our rite*
> *As You travel back home, please encourage the Light*
> *To grow and be strong, and warm this home we call Earth*
> *We bid You farewell in love, laughter, and mirth*

Dismiss the other guardians in the same manner, traveling to the south, the west, and finishing at the northern quarter. Release the Circle in your usual manner using the oak leaf in place of the holly sprig. (For especially good luck throughout the coming year, store a piece of the leaf with the ashes you collect.)

WINTER SOLSTICE PURGING

(Contributed by Jami Shoemaker)

Because Yule truly exemplifies the adage, "The greatest darkness comes before dawn," it may be seen as an opportunity to embrace the darkness one last time before the growing light takes hold. In doing so, we also present ourselves with something else just as important: A time to purge ourselves of that which is no longer useful, and an opportunity to make room to receive all the gifts of the returning light.

PURGING RITUAL

Metal cauldron
Charcoal lighter fluid
Matches or cigarette lighter
Scraps of paper and writing tools*

Gather around the cauldron (the Transformative Void of the Mother) and talk about the aspects of darkness and all that they signify. Then think about the dead weight in your life—the useless things you wish to get rid of—any negative aspects that you wish to transform into something more positive. During this process, remember that banished aspects are often replaced with their exact opposites, so it's a good idea to consider whether you're ready to admit those into your life.

Once you've decided what needs to go, write the objectives on scraps of paper and place them in the cauldron with purpose and concentration. Know that by releasing them into the cauldron, you are pulling them out of your own darkness to make way for the gifts of light.

Sprinkle the papers liberally with lighter fluid while concentrating on the transformative qualities of the cauldron. Light the fire knowing that all that is released into darkness is transformed by light. Let the papers burn to ash, then release them on the wind.

*The type of paper and color of ink used can be highly significant. If your intent is to purge yourself of poverty, for example, you might write your message on an old bank statement in large, bold letters. On the other hand, red lettering on the photo of an ex-love might be appropriate if you wish to release the passion you still feel for the person and transform it into energy of a more positive nature.

DECEMBER 22

In some countries, today is Children's Day. (Others celebrate this holiday on December 25.) The origins of this event had to do with the fact that children are symbolic of the Yule Child; thus, they are the warmth and promise of our world. Join in the celebration by spending some time with your own children or neighborhood youngsters. Play games. Give them treats. Encourage them in their endeavors and build their self-confidence. Before you go to bed at night, say the following prayer for the children of the world.

Ancient Ones from near and far
Protect our children from all war
Give them peace, and hope, and love
And clean air that blows free from above
A world with fish, and trees, and Sun
Where they are safe when day is done
Watch over them and guide them, please
As I will, so mote it be

DECEMBER 23

Today marks the last day of the Roman year at which time the Festivals of Laurentia (The Patroness of Death, The Old Year, and Life to Come) and Lares (the ancestors) are celebrated. to make it special, look back on important personal events that happened over the last year, then say your farewells. You may wish to close the old year by saying something like:

With fondest memories, I let you go
Ride the changing winds that blow
I'll not forget the fun we had
But I release all things that made me sad
I wish you well as you fly out
Old Year, I'll miss you—there's no doubt

It's also a good time to get rid of any dark spots in your life. Begin by holding a small amethyst in your hand. Then close your eyes and go deep within yourself. Take a look at what's there, and closely examine any unsavory character traits or painful experiences. Visualize them leaving your spirit and traveling into the amethyst. Then honor your ancestors by asking their help to clean up any leftover fragments that may be hanging on. Enlist their help by chanting something like:

Foremothers and fathers, hear my plea
Of darkness, let my life be free
Pack away those things that hurt
And clear out all the dust and dirt
So that white light may shine in me
As I will, so mote it be

DECEMBER 24

Because the Finnish people believe that the spirits of the dead revisit their old homes on this day, they light white candles on graves to help them find their way. To honor those who once lived in your home, light a white candle and enchant it by saying something like:

Spirits, you are welcome here
Rejoin this home and have no fear
We're glad to have you—you may stay
Until you need to fly away

The Celtic Tree Month of Beth also begins today. This month—dedicated to the birch tree—symbolizes birth and purification. For that reason, it's a great time to get rid of the old and make room for the new. Start the day with a spiritually purifying salt bath. Run a tub of hot water, toss in a handful of salt, and say something like:

Salt of power, salt of might
Rid my life of what's not right
Release all negativity
Cleanse me now, salt. Blessed be

DECEMBER 25

For a good portion of the world's population, today is Christmas, the birthday of the Christ-child. However, other Sun Deities share this birthday, too—Sol Ivictus and Horus, just to name a couple. This day also marks Haloa, a threshing festival that celebrates the birth of Dionysus, the God of Wine and Grain. So how do you honor each of Them without spreading yourself too thin? Go outside and toast all the Sun Deities with a glass of hot lemonade. Say something like:

Gods of Sun, come One and All
Goddesses, too—now hear our call
Grow and shine up in the sky
Warm our planet from on high
Cast Your rays upon us, too
As we drink this glass to honor You

DECEMBER 26

Today is St. Stephen's Day, and in ancient times it was customary to hunt the wren in celebration. Wrens were captured, put in a box, and called, "King." Children then took the birds from house to house while singing a little ditty and begging for treats. Because this practice was a bit barbaric, it's now celebrated throughout Europe by suspending a toy bird from a stick to avoid harming our feathered friends. Instead of hunting the wren today, spend some time feeding the birds or making them peanut butter cakes (see directions in the Gift Section). As you distribute the cakes or scatter the seeds, say something like:

Feathered friends, come one and all
Both thin and fat, both large and small
These treats of love we leave for you
With many thanks for all you do

This is also the day that many cultures participate in something called Boxing Day. Originally, this was the time that British employers gave holiday gifts to their staff members. Today, though, it's become an event to collect money and gifts for the less fortunate. Since it's not feasible to collect door-to-door, go through closets and toy boxes for items you no longer need. Box them up and deliver them to the nearest Salvation Army, GoodWill, or another charitable organization.

DECEMBER 27

The birthday of Freya—the Norse Goddess of Love for which Friday is named—is celebrated on this day. Since matters of the heart are Her business, it's a good time to perform any magical efforts involving love—unconditional or otherwise. Get your family in on the act by serving them "love" foods like baked apples, cinnamon candies, or cherry pie. Then ask them to join you in the following prayer to Freya for family love throughout the coming year.

Freya, Goddess of Perfect Love
Shine upon us from Your throne above
Your tenderness, please grant us each
Please bring Your love within our reach
And let it grow and swell in us
Overpowering all that makes us fuss
So that we live in harmony
And perfect love—so mote it be

DECEMBER 28

On this day, the Chinese hold a festival of peace, spiritual enlightenment, and renewal. Many offerings are made to the Deities, and among them is a paper horse holding the names of all the festival participants. The horse is set on fire in hopes that the names will fly into the heavens on the rising smoke and be recognized by the Ancients. Follow suit by writing wishes for the world on paper and burning them. Some ideas might include world peace, the eradication of disease, or the renewal of our planet.

Today is also Bairns Day, and in many countries, it's believed that it's unlucky to do any work. Keeping that in mind, use today to do something nice for yourself. Give yourself a treat and invite your favorite Deities to join in the fun.

DECEMBER 29

This is the day I usually dedicate to my pets, two labrador retrievers named Sadie and Jonah. I bathe them, groom them, and give them an extra large dose of tender loving care. They sleep in the bed, lie around on the furniture, and for all practical purposes, become human beings for the day. I also bake their favorite treats. (See the Dog Biscuit recipe in Chapter 16.) Before I go to bed at night, I slip a new hematite ring on their collars and say the following prayer of protection to Diana.

O Great Diana, to You I pray
Keep my dogs out of harm's way
Keep them always safe and warm
Preserve their health, and with this charm
Keep them under Your protection
I ask You this with love and affection

If there are cats in your household, don't despair. Treat them with a kitty toy. (For instructions, see the Quick and Easy Yule Gifts section.)

DECEMBER 30

I like to call this Thank-You Day. It provides a great time to settle in and write thank-you notes for holiday gifts. I usually take this a step further, though. Fact is, I'm a firm believer in giving "flowers" to the living—so on this day I celebrate other people. I make it a point to remind them how their existence has changed my life and how much they mean to me. When celebrating this day, don't forget a special vote of thanks to the Ancients. Honor Them by lighting a yellow candle and saying something like:

Ancient Ones from far and near
Come forward now and bend an ear
I thank You for the roles you play
In getting me through every day
For providing opportunities
For lessons learned and lessons eased
For wrapping me within Your love
And guiding me from up above
For all the little things You do
For these and more, I cherish You

December 31

The last day of the year is dedicated to Hogmagog, the Sun God. Shortly before midnight, join the Scottish by opening all the doors and windows to rid your home of the spirits of the old year. As you open them, shoo the spirits out by chanting something like:

Spirits of cold and darkness, go
Your time here is spent—fly out high and low
Clear out of this house and make room for the new
Take your leave now—I bid you adieu

Even though the event calendar ends here, nothing says your holiday celebration has to. For other ideas, check the Internet or your public library. Use your imagination and exercise your creative flow. You'll be able to find any number of reasons to celebrate throughout the winter—reasons to warm your heart and spirit, and bring light to the world you live in.

19

Keeping the Holidays Happy

No matter how festive the winter holidays are or how much we look forward to them, they have a flip side that affects thousands of people every year. It starts out with stress and works its way into anxiety. Sometimes, it grows and grows until we find ourselves completely overwhelmed. That's when depression rears its ugly head, and once it takes hold, we're often just too tired to shake it off. We spend the bulk of the holiday season in emotional turmoil, and that's just no way to celebrate.

No one is safe from the spoils of depression. It pulls no punches and can affect anyone—even positive thinkers like you and me. For this reason, we need to take some preventative measures to ensure that it doesn't corrupt our celebration or ruin our fun. Following the short list of anti-anxiety essentials below will definitely hold depression at bay—and guarantee that your holiday not only begins on a celebratory note, but ends that way as well!

- Don't try to do everything in one day. Do what you can and save the rest for tomorrow.

- If you're still overwhelmed, ask for help. Since this is a time of cheer and good will, family, friends, and neighbors will be delighted to come to your aid.

- Laugh loud and often—especially at yourself. Because your to-do list is hefty this time of year, you're bound to screw up or make a mistake now and then. Laughter is great medicine for this. It renews the stamina and provides the personal force necessary to right what's wrong and move forward.

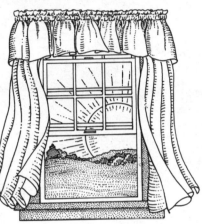

- Avoid shopping malls during the holiday season if crowds make you anxious. Either shop early, use mailorder, or *make* necessary gifts instead.

- Open the drapes or blinds. Natural light is a terrific antidepressant. Besides, letting in a little light is a great way to encourage the birth of the Sun.

- Even if you don't see yourself as much of a party animal, make it a point to accept invitations. It's hard to be depressed when in the company of a group of fun-loving party-goers.

- Take some time each day to do something nice for yourself. This can take any form at all—from a long, hot, candlelit bath to time out for a hot mug of gourmet coffee. Rewarding yourself is an excellent anxiety deterrent; besides, after working so hard to make the holidays special for everyone else, you definitely deserve a treat!

20

AFTER THE HOLIDAYS

MANY PEOPLE DREAD THE END of the winter holidays. It's not for the reasons you might think, though. They dread it because everything related to the celebratory period—decorations, ornaments, stockings, and so on—must be taken down, packed up, and put away. It's tiring, time-consuming work. Couple that with a shortage of storage space, and the problem snowballs into something else entirely—a royal pain.

For this reason, I've included some time-saving tips and ideas to help solve your storage problems and give you a head start for next year's festivities. Give them a shot. You'll be kicking back with a hot mug of apple cider long before your neighbors have even figured out a game plan!

• Remove artificial snow spray from windows with an ice scraper, then wipe away any residue with rubbing alcohol and newspaper.

- Use clear plastic tubs with snap-on lids to store artificial trees, ornaments, light strands, and decorations. They not only stack well, but next year, you'll be able to see what's inside before you dig through it.

- Wind tinsel garlands and light strands around old gift wrap tubes, and secure the ends with tape. This keeps lights from getting tangled, but the help goes further than that: Next year, just remove the tape from the plug end, then try it in the outlet before you unwind it. You'll be able to easily identify which bulbs need replacements.

- Don't toss cranberry, popcorn, or seed garlands. Hang them outside for the birds, instead. (Fences and tree branches are good bets.) After the birds have had their feast, cut the threads into small lengths (six to eight inches) and scatter them on the ground. The birds will use them for nest-building materials when spring comes.

- Don't throw away used foil icicles. Instead, gather them into bundles and secure them with twist-ties, then store them in plastic zippered bags. You can transform them into doorknob tassels or twist them into napkin rings for next year's holiday.

- Use styrofoam peanuts, old newspaper, and leftover gift tissue to wrap glass ornaments or other breakables when packing them away for storage.

- Protect and preserve children's paper holiday art pieces by spraying them liberally with clear art spray or shellac.

- Wrap paper ornaments in acid paper before storing them. This protects them from becoming yellowed and brittle.

- Gather the envelopes from the holiday cards you received and put them in alphabetical order. Secure the bundle with a rubber band, toss it in a zippered bag, and pack away with paper decorations. Next year, you'll have a handy list when it's time to send holiday cards.

- Put name tags from the gifts you received in an envelope and pack them away, too. When you make up next year's gift list, you'll be sure no one is forgotten.

- Once everything is put away, grab some paper and a pen. Jot down new ideas that you tried this year. Make notations of what worked for you, what didn't, and what you might like to try next year. Then sort through your holiday photos. Pick out the really good ones and put them in a scrapbook. Place the list in the scrapbook, along with any comments you may have about this year's festivities. Add related anecdotes and stories, swatches of exceptionally pretty gift wrap and ribbon, or any other meaningful items. Sign your  name and date it when you're finished. Put the book in a safe place and add to it each year. It's the best way I know to pass on personal holiday traditions and memories to future generations.

Charge of the Sun God

I am the Light that bursts through the Darkness
And the smile on the young child's face
I am the warmth that melts the winter chill
And the sparks that dance from the old fireplace
I am the smell of oranges and apples
And the scent of cinnamon, nutmeg, and clove
I am the holly, the ivy, the mistletoe ball,
And the jocularity of the Great God, Jove
I am found in the twinkling of an aged eye
And in the hope of children everywhere
Yes, joy and love and warmth am I
Where kindness abounds, I, too, am there
I am your brother, your father, the wise one
And I warm you gently in the light of my love.
I lighten your worries, bring good health and speed growth
By shedding my rays down on you from above
But remember, my children, be grateful
For my brother, the Darkness, and winter's deep chill
For without them, there would be little reason
For this holiday season of peace and good will

—Dorothy Morrison

APPENDIX I
GODDESSES ASSOCIATED WITH YULE

Alcyone

Amaterasu

Astraea

Babouschka

Bamya

Bertha

Black Madonna

Bona Dea

Bruma

Cailleach Bheur

Demeter

Eguski

Frigg

Freya

Hertha

Holle

Isis

Lady of Guadalupe

Liberty

La Befana

Lucina

Mary

ModresNach

Mother Night

Mudda Nacht

Ncith

Ops

Pallas Athena

Perchta

Rhea

Sankrat

Sapientia

Sephira

Skadi

Sophia

Spider Woman

Takel

Tonatzin

Unchi-Ahchi

Xi Hou

Appendix II
Gods Associated with Yule

Apollo

Attis

Babbo Natale

Balder

Black Peter

Bozicek

Chango

Cronos

Ded Moroz

Diev

Dionysus

Dun Che Lao Ren

Father Sun

Father Winter

Hercules

Hogmagog

Holly King

Horned One

Horus

Jesus

St. Nicholas

Saturn

Sinterklaas

Shengdan Laoren

Sin dan lo ian

Sol Ivictus

Joulupukki

Julbocken

Julgubben

Julenissen

Juliman

Jupiter

Karascony Apo

Kerstman

Kris Kringle

Lord of Misrule

Marduk

Mithra

Oak King

Odin

Osris

Papai Noel

Pere Noel

Perseus

Ra

Santa Claus

Theseus

Thor

Woden

Zeus

Ziemmassve'tku veci'tis

Appendix III
Holiday Greetings in Other Countries

Africa: Rehus-Beal-Ledeats

Albania: Gezur Krislinjden

Argentina: Feliz Navidad

Brazil: Boas Festas e Feliz Ano Novo

Bulgaria: Tchestita Koleda; Tchestito Rojdestvo Hristovo

Croatia: Sretan Bozic

Czechoslovakia: Prejeme Vam Vesele Vanoce a stastny Novy Rok

Finland: Hyvaa Joulua

France: Joyeux Noel

Germany: Froehliche Weihnachten

Greece: Kala Christouyenna

Holland: Vrolijk Kerstfeest en een Gelukkig Nieuwjaar

Hungary: Kellemes Karacsonyi Unnepeket

Iceland: Gledileg Jol

Indonesia: Selamat Hari Natal

Iraq: Idah Saidan Wa Sanah Jadidah

Ireland: Nollaig Shona Dhuit; Nodlaig mhaith chugnat

Italy: Buone Feste natalizie

Japan: Shinnen Omedeto; Kurisumasu Omedeto

Latvia: Prieci'gus Ziemsve'tkus un Laimi'gu Januno Gadu

Norway: God Jul; Gledelig Jul

Rumania: Sarbatori vesele

Russia: Pozdrevlyayu s prazdnikom Roxhdestva is Novim Godom

Scotland: Nollaig chridheil huibh

Spain: Feliz Navidad

Sweden: God Jul; Ett Gott Nytt Ar

Thailand: Sawadee Pee Mai

Turkey: Noeliniz Ve Yeni Yiliniz Kutlu Olsun

Wales: Nadolig Llawen

Yugoslavia: Cestitamo Bozic

Yoruba: E Ku odun e ku iye'dun

Appendix IV
Yule-Related Websites

http://www.algonet.se/~bernadot/christmas/

http://www.argyll.demon.co.uk/xmas.html

http://www.candlegrove.com/yule.html

http://www.circlesanctuary.org/pholidays/

http://www.cvc.org/christmas/#history

http://www.infidels.org/org/aha/ceremonies/meaning-christmas.html

http://www.infostarbase.com/tnr/xmas/santa.html

http://www.imagitek.com/xmas

http://www.oakridger.com/stories/122297/aps_legacy.html

http://www.maui.net/~mcculc/xmas.htm

http://www.polishworld.com/christmas/

http://www.prime.org/holiday/xmas1.html

http://www.santas.net

http://www.the-north-pole.com

http://www.santaclaus.com

Bibliography

Campanelli, Pauline. *Wheel of the Year: Living the Magical Life.* Saint Paul, MN: Llewellyn Publications, 1989.

Conway, D. J. *Ancient Shining Ones.* Saint Paul, MN: Llewellyn Publications, 1993.

Cooper, J. C. *The Aquarian Dictionary of Festivals.* Northamptonshire, England: Aquarian Press, a subsidiary of Thorson's Publishing Group, 1990.

Cross, Jean. *Granny's Recipes, Remedies, and Helpful Hints.* New York: Weathervane Books, 1989.

Henderson, Henele, and Sue Ellen Thompson, eds, *Holidays, Festivals, and Celebrations of the World Dictionary.* Detroit, MI: Omnigraphics, 1997.

J. C. Penney Co. *Handmade from the Heart: Creative Crafts for all Seasons.* Kearney, NE: Morris Publishing, 1996.

Monaghan, Patricia. *Goddesses & Heroines.* Saint Paul, MN: Llewellyn Publications, 1998.

New LaRosse Encyclopedia of Mythology. Middlesex, England: Hamlin Publishers, 1968.

Petrash, Carol. *Earthways.* Mt. Rainier, MD: Gryphon House, Inc., 1992.

Polley, Jane, ed. *Reader's Digest American Folklore and Legend.* Pleasantville, N.Y.: Reader's Digest Association, Inc., 1978.

Rufus, Anneli. *The World Holiday Book.* San Francisco: Harper San Franciso, 1994.

Stein, Diane. *The Goddess Book of Days.* Saint Paul, MN: Llewellyn Publications, 1998; Freedom, CA: Crossing Press, 1992.

Telesco, Patricia. *365 Goddess: A Daily Guide to the Magic and Inspiration of the Goddess.* New York: Harper San Francisco, a Division of Harper Collins, 1998.

van Renterghem, Tony. *When Santa was a Shaman.* Saint Paul, MN: Llewellyn Publications, 1995.

Walker, Barbara G. *The Woman's Encyclopedia of Myths and Secrets.* New York: Harper & Rowe Publishers, Inc., 1983.

Index

Halloween
Customs, Recipes & Spells

Silver RavenWolf

Grab your flowing cape and journey through the history and magickal practices of America's favorite scary holiday. From Old World roots to New World charm, you will traverse the hodgepodge of legends and customs that created our modern tradition. *Halloween* brings you serious facts based on accurate research, as well as practical, how-to goodies and gossipy tidbits. Learn how history created many inaccurate myths about the original Halloween, which the ancient Celts called "Samhain," and how modern pagans still view it as a religious celebration. Discover practices, rituals, and recipes that honor the spirit of the holiday, which you can adapt to fit any spiritual orientation.

1-56718-719-6
264 pp., 7½ x 9⅛, illus.   **$12.95**

In Praise of the Crone
A Celebration of Feminine Maturity

Dorothy Morrison

When Dorothy Morrison began her menopausal metamorphosis at the early age of 32, she thought her life was over. Then she discovered a reason to celebrate: she'd been invited to the Crone's party!

Meet your hostess and mentor, your Personal Crone. Mingle a bit and find your Spirit Self. Discover why the three of you belong together. Learn to balance yourself, gather wisdom, reclaim your life, and make the most of your natural beauty. Then meander into the Crone's kitchen and find home remedies that can take the edge off minor menopausal aggravations without the use of hormone replacement therapy or prescription drugs.

Written with humor and compassion from someone who's been there, In Praise of the Crone alleviates the negativity and fear surrounding menopause with a wealth of meditations, invocations, rituals, spells, chants, songs, recipes, and other tips that will help you successfully face your own emotional and spiritual challenges.

1-56718-468-5
288 pp., 6 x 9 $14.95

Everyday Magic
Spells & Rituals for Modern Living

DOROTHY MORRISON

Are you tired of looking for ritual solutions for today's problems: computer viruses, traffic that drives you crazy, and stress that makes you forget your own name? Does the quest for obscure spell ingredients leave you exhausted and empty-handed?

Now there's a better way to incorporate magic into your life without adding more stress to it. Everyday Magic updates the ancient arts to fit today's lifestyle. It promotes the use of modern convenience items as viable magical tools, and it incorporates the use of easy-to-find spell ingredients—most of which are already in your kitchen cabinet. It discusses the items and forces that boost magical work, as well as a multitude of time-saving tips and a large assortment of recipes for creating your own oils, incenses, potions, and powders. More than 300 spells and rituals cover the everyday concerns of the modern practitioner.

1-56718-469-3
304 pp., 5³⁄₁₆ x 8 $9.95

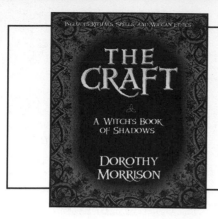

The Craft
A Witch's Book of Shadows

Dorothy Morrison

Teaching newcomers how to begin the path of the witch . . .

So, you want to be a witch. You've read everything you can get your hands on about spells and magic, but you're still asking yourself, "How do I begin?"

The Craft answers that question, and so many more. Beginning with the basics of the Wiccan religion and its practices, this book moves forward with easy-to-follow instructions for working with major power sources like the Deities and Elements. You'll discover the importance of magical boosters, and find out how to get the most from their power. You'll travel the path of ritual tools, and learn to make, obtain, and use them to their best advantage. Then it's off to Circle-casting, and all it has to offer. Afterward, you'll explore the realm of the Esbats, the Sabbats, and the party-hardy world of ritual celebration. Everything you need for successful witchery is here, including mental theory, magical theory, and practical training exercises.

- Gives 'tweens, teens, and those new to the Craft a solid, but basic set of instructions and guidelines for beginning their practice of the Ancient Arts

- Discusses the Wiccan religion and its belief system with a detailed listing of its laws, rules, and principles

- Shows how to make/obtain and use basic tools of the Craft, complete with related consecrations, tool exercises, and magical theories

- Gives easy-to-follow instructions for altar setup, circle-casting, building power, Deity invocation, and more

1-56718-446-4
7½ x 9⅛, 240 pp., illus.

$14.95

To order, call 1-877-NEW-WRLD

Prices subject to change without notice

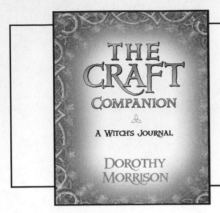

The Craft Companion
A Witch's Journal

DOROTHY MORRISON

Craft your own Book of Shadows . . .

Start your own Book of Shadows with this companion guide to *The Craft. The Craft Companion's* journal-like format with lined pages gives you plenty of room for your own magical notes and planning. A unique assortment of more than 100 short spells and affirmations, one per each journal page, are designed to spark creativity and further you along the spiritual path. Also includes the Wiccan Rede.

One example is a helpful spell for business agreements:

> For success on contracts signed—
> Or written papers of any kind—
> Turn the papers all face down
> And with each one a pentacle crown
> Just lick your finger and then draw
> Then bind the spell with Karmic Law

0-7387-0093-2
240 pp., 7 ½ x 9 ⅛

$14.95